302.343 Wood, Leslie Anne.
WOO     Bullied But Not Beaten

©2013

# *Bullied But Not Beaten!*

## Years of Torment and Threats of Murder Reveal Ways to Combat Bullying

## Leslie Anne Wood

ST. MARY PARISH LIBRARY
FRANKLIN, LOUISIANA

Copyright ©2012 by Leslie Anne Wood

All rights reserved

This publication may not be reproduced, stored in a retrieval system, or transmitted in whole or in part in any form or by any means, electronic, mechanical, photocopying, recording or otherwise without the prior written permission of Leslie A. Wood

This story is based on true events. The names of people, places and dates have been changed to protect the privacy of those involved.

Published by NewInsight Publications, LLC, Mesa AZ

Wood, Leslie Anne

*Bullied but Not Beaten*

1. Bullying.  2. Peer Victimization.  3. Peer Aggression.
4. Cyber-bullying,  5. Bully Prevention.  6. Sports Bullying.
7. Parenting.

ISBN 978-0-9701642-3-0

Printing Number  10 9 8 7 6 5 4 3 2 1

# Acknowledgements

THIS BOOK IS DEDICATED TO the many friends and loved ones who helped me along the way. To my daughter, who inspires me with her strength and perseverance in all things. To my friends Greg and Margaret, thank you for standing strong at my side while I walked in the darkness of this bullying experience. To Virginia, who chidingly told me to "get back to work!" (finish the book), after all of our phone visits. And to Milton, for his help as a reader, editor and in the summarization of "Lessons Learned." I love you all.

# Contents

Author's Note ............................... vii
Introduction ................................. ix
Chapter 1   Camp and More ..................... 1
Chapter 2   Achieving Goals ................... 5
Chapter 3   Success in the Pool ............... 9
Chapter 4   Moving Up in the World of
            Swimming ......................... 17
Chapter 5   The 5A Championships ............. 25
Chapter 6   The Letterman's Jacket ........... 35
Chapter 7   Bodyguard ........................ 41
Chapter 8   Prison Break ..................... 55
Chapter 9   Angelic Surprise ................. 59
Chapter 10  The Tough Go Shopping ............ 67
Chapter 11  Moving to Gilmore ................ 73

| | | |
|---|---|---|
| Chapter 12 | A Fresh Start | 83 |
| Chapter 13 | A New Team | 95 |
| Chapter 14 | Junior Nationals | 105 |
| Chapter 15 | Facing Weighty Issues | 115 |
| Chapter 16 | Transition | 121 |
| Chapter 17 | Senior Year | 125 |
| Chapter 18 | New Beginnings | 133 |
| Chapter 19 | Lessons Learned | 137 |
| Chapter 20 | Epilogue | 147 |
| Appendix | Recent Research | 149 |

# Author's Note

THIS BOOK HAS BEEN in my head for several years. I knew it would be written someday, but it was unclear to me when that would happen. It took that much time for the people in this real-life story to heal emotionally and be able to speak the truth without unbearable pain.

There was something about the picture of Phoebe Prince, and her 2010 obituary, that made me understand that now was the time to write "our" story. I cut out the article about Phoebe and I have it with me as I write. Maybe it was her picture, but something reminded me of my own beloved child who might have become another statistic.

As I researched other young people who chose suicide as the only escape from bullying, I was stunned by the number of case histories I found. To remain in touch with those young people I often look at their pictures and read their stories. I cannot fathom the pain of losing a beloved child; but, I can say that I have witnessed and experienced the pain of watching a loved one be bullied emotionally, physically and mentally, all in the name of sports. My child was a victim of property theft, personal attack, and loss of self-worth, all because of the selfish, brutal acts of others who "pretended" to be friends.

I asked my daughter for her blessing before I began to write our painful story. She was touched that I would do so and encouraged me to carry on. All the names have been changed including my own. There will be some who remember me by my first name and that is not a problem. What they should remember is one devoted mother fighting for her only child. To protect her from any delayed bullying I will call her Celeste. Thirty years later, I still wonder about the possibility of retaliation.

It is my heartfelt desire to honor those young people who chose suicide as their only option. I offer my sincerest sympathy to their grieving families. This is the reason that our story must be written; to keep these senseless tragedies from happening again and again. If my writing saves one young person, or helps others manage the bullying process, this book will have been a success.

# Introduction

THE DARKEST HOUR OF MY LIFE did not come between the hours of midnight and dawn. It happened on a Friday afternoon after a celebratory morning.

The day before, I had interceded on behalf of my fifteen year old daughter Celeste who had been bullied relentlessly for two years. The reason for the mistreatment by coaches, teachers and teammates was nothing more than selfishness and petty jealousy, all because she was a gifted and talented swimmer. The fact that she was pretty and petite only exacerbated the situation.

I had always believed that Celeste should fight her own battles. At the same time I always tried to be a supportive, yet unobtrusive mother. I encouraged and attended any and all events that interested her; both scholastic, individual, as well as her team sports.

I was told by her teachers and coaches that she was a natural athlete and could succeed in any sport she chose. I believed what they said because I had watched her swim at the age of two, ride her bike with ease and become actively involved in sports through grade school and beyond. She had always enjoyed sports camps in grade school and seemed happiest when participating in outdoor activities.

At age thirteen my daughter needed to make some tough choices. Celeste was excelling at both ballet and swimming, showing us that she was ready for the next level in each sport. This would require serious time expenditures, not only from her but our entire family as well. Without any prompting from us, she decided that she would pursue swimming. She based her decision on the fact that dancers are known to have long-term troubles with their feet. She wanted no part of that problem.

At that time I had no idea what lay ahead in the world of swimming. I was naïve about the world of sports in general and the pressures that elite athletes face every day. My background was in music and education; I had never excelled or pushed myself in the world of competitive sports.

Our lives changed forever the summer she started to swim on a local team. The story you are about to read describes the events, situations and emotional highs and lows she experienced while moving ahead in the world of competitive team sports. The choice to compete as a swimmer seemed exciting at the time; but, it quickly changed into a world of darkness that none of us had anticipated.

## Chapter One
# Camp and More

OUR DAUGHTER, who loved summer sports camps, attended her first western riding camp when she was eleven. My husband and I decided that our only child needed that first adventure away from the daily routine of Mom and Dad. Celeste was excited about her upcoming experience, but I saw a look of "panic" on her face as she boarded a bus for the two hour ride to camp. I knew she would experience a stab of home sickness as she left home and family behind, so I made certain there was a tasty package waiting for her when she arrived. Unfortunately, many children get "shipped off" to camp so parents can get some time off. This was not the purpose behind this trip; it was for her to experience her own independence and for me to begin "letting go" of my quickly maturing daughter.

During the month she was gone, I busied myself painting and redecorating her room. I was intent upon changing its "look" from "small child" to "growing young woman." As I worked in her room painting walls and furniture, changing bedspreads and putting up new wallpaper, I felt a definite connection with my child. I missed her terribly, but I did not want her to know. In an attempt to manage my loneliness I wrote her uplifting letters about things happening at home, making sure to keep her updated regarding her pets and family activities.

Unfortunately, she felt completely disconnected from us. We got sad letters from the "Unhappy Trails Camp," her made-up return address. Because I was a bit concerned, I made secretive calls to the camp director who assured me that she was getting along just fine. When we visited her on Parents' Weekend, we helped her understand that she needed to finish her time there without giving up. That seemed to be a "theme" in my parenting style that lasted throughout her childhood. "Honor your commitments" was my message. I was not going to allow an eleven-year-old to have her way because she didn't like it there.

She struggled through the month and so did I. When her dad and I finally picked her up it was a wonderful reunion for all of us. We even took her a brand new outfit to wear home. As we ate lunch before the drive home she pleaded, "Mom and Dad, I did what you told me to do; but, please don't ever send me there again."

Hmmm. My child seemed to be as willful as her mother! We would have to wait a year until the topic would come up again.

The school year passed quickly. After the sixth grade, it was time to think about summer activities. She was still standing firm on the "no return" policy toward camp. My answer to this was, "Well, if you are not going to camp, then you are going to swim on the local swim team and take ballet as well. You will not be spending all summer in front of the television."

Celeste was delighted to stay home and started swim practice with an upbeat attitude. The coach of the team was happy to have her on board. Since she had been in the pool since the age of two, Celeste was a strong and capable swimmer. Her confidence grew as we attended meets in the eastern part of our large metropolitan city. During the last meet of the summer, she helped her team make the finals by placing in the freestyle, backstroke and the butterfly. There was only one young woman who could beat her. This talented young lady won all three events in their twelve to thirteen age group. I could see the look in Celeste's eye, "Next year I will beat you!" She had a competitive attitude and I was one proud mother.

## Chapter Two

## *Achieving Goals*

During the following school year, **Celeste** continued with dance classes. Her ballet instructor's name was Ms. Karen, a well-known local teacher who had danced with several national ballet companies before forming her own company. She was an elite athlete herself. To no one's surprise, she expected a lot from Celeste; however, she also nurtured the natural talent that our daughter seemed to possess. When Celeste began to outgrow the beginning class, Ms. Karen suggested that she transfer to one of her more advanced training companies on the opposite side of town. I was willing to make the drive, yet Celeste was hesitant. She seemed to like being the "big fish in a little pond." This allowed her to perform without the pressure of being the best. Much to Celeste's chagrin, I supported her teacher in this contest of wills. I reminded Celeste that her teacher was the professional and knew what was best for her students. I said, "Let's just try this. If it is not for you, then you can move back to the smaller group." Not fully convinced, Celeste agreed.

With all of this on again, off again activity, I was pleased to have the opportunity to physically "be there" for my child as she faced these decisions. If I had been working as a full-time teacher I would not have had the flexibility I had as a substitute teacher. Having worked as both a kindergarten and pre-school teacher when Celeste was very small, I had learned how much time and effort a good job of teaching required. However, as a substitute, I could leave immediately and not have the responsibilities of a full-time contract teacher. As a result, I promised myself that I would be there to support my daughter's efforts until she started college. Each day that I picked her up from school and drove her to all of her after-school activities I was honoring my own commitment. As it turned out, the two of us followed this routine until she was eighteen and on her way to higher education.

The first day Celeste started training with her new ballet group, we took great care to do her hair right and have all of the appropriate ballet clothing. When Celeste joined the class it did not go unnoticed that some "new kid" had suddenly arrived from "out of the blue." To say the least, the atmosphere toward Celeste was "chilly" at best. I stayed until practice began and then left to let her cope on her own. When I returned, I saw that same look of "panic" on her face that I had seen on the bus ride to camp: "Mom! I hate it here! Everyone is mean and they expect too much from me!"

Well, this "honor your commitments" mom was not going to let her quit right away. I made her "tough it out" for a month since it was close to the end of the school year and the swim season was right around the corner. As we talked about whether or not she would continue ballet, Celeste decided she had gone as far as she wanted to go in dance. She realized that she had outgrown her original beginner group and was unwilling to continue with the more advanced classes. At this point in their training, most of them were dancing en pointe (toe shoes). She knew this would be expected of her soon. The fact that ballet dancers can have serious foot problems, in combination with her hard-to-fit feet, convinced us that ballet was no longer a good choice for her.

As she approached the end of the seventh grade, she decided she wanted to re-join the local swim team. She looked forward to seeing all of her friends again and taking part in the fun they had together. I also knew she was looking forward to winning in her age group and taking home that trophy that had eluded her the summer before.

I continued my role as the supportive mom, remaining firm in my effort to keep her busy. As a teacher I had found that the "busy" child is usually the one who stays out of trouble and I adopted that philosophy to use with my own child.

## Chapter Three
# Success in the Pool

SWIM PRACTICE AT THE BEGINNING LEVEL was fun and productive. The swimmers on Celeste's team met at our neighborhood pool and worked out for two hours in the morning. It was enjoyable for all of the swimmers because the coaches made it fun for them to be there each day. The exercise wore them out, so they were more pleasant teens in the afternoon. All of the parents were grateful for this small favor!

The age range of the swimmers was from five to thirteen. The program was organized so that swimmers competed with those in their own age group. The head coach was a formidable man of considerable size; a man who was once a swimmer, but was now a body builder and swim coach. He had two young assistants just out of high school. All of the coaches had achieved some level of success in competitive swimming; but, I was unsure how successful they had been. Actually, it didn't matter. This was all about having a good time and improving stroke technique. I was particularly pleased that "good sportsmanship" was an important part of their agenda.

It was that year, at age thirteen, that Celeste seemed to take off in the pool. She was a little slow off the blocks, (her starts), but all of the swimmers seemed to have the same problem. One of the problems was simple concentration. As I watched each of the swimmers standing on the blocks ready to race, their minds seemed to be elsewhere...not completely focused on the start.

The "middle school" years were a challenging time for sure. We managed to survive, parents and children alike, but they were painful years at best. Fortunately, watching my daughter perform helped me cope with some of the ups and downs that every family experienced.

The coaches worked hard to improve Celeste's technique in the water. She had a very unusual underwater "pull," as well as tremendous strength in her upper body. Her swimming stroke seemed to come naturally and the added pull contributed to her success at the swim meets. Each time she neared the finish line she was able to turn on the power, just in time to win the race. It quickly became apparent that freestyle was her favorite stroke, probably because she excelled at it. She also "anchored" (swam last) in all of the relays. Her ability to provide an amazing final burst of speed won many of the relays, even if her team was laps behind when it was her turn to finish the race.

## Chapter 3: Success in the Pool

If you would like a mental picture of my child, imagine the opposite of a powerfully built, six-foot, European farm girl. Celeste was "powerfully built," but she was a small powerhouse who never grew taller than five-foot-three-and-three-quarter inches in height. She has maintained her sturdy, yet petite figure to this day.

The official meets were held against other swimmers in our local metropolitan area. This was summer "league" swimming and anyone could be part of the team. Because the meets were held in the evening, Celeste's dad could go with us and enjoy watching his daughter excel in the pool.

Her dad enjoyed the competition because he was a formidable force in the world of shooting sports himself. He once qualified as a member of the USA International Trap and Skeet Olympic Team. As a world class athlete, he enjoyed seeing his child continuing a "winning" tradition. There seemed to be a competitive "gene" from both sides of our family. My father had been a successful swimmer in high school and Ben's mother was a talented equestrian. Celeste had been gifted with a "double" dose of talent and endurance.

The social aspects of being part of the team suited Celeste just fine. She loved having girlfriends to chat and share time with outside of swim practice. It seemed our only daughter was very gregarious child. She was never a "lonely only." From the time she was a toddler, she never played well by herself, so we had a constant stream of young people coming and going during her "at home" years. Our social butterfly was only happy when "connected" to others her own age.

The end of July brought the final meet where Celeste would face-off against the young woman who had beaten her the year before. This was a challenging competition because only the fastest swimmers from all the age groups were allowed to compete. Celeste had quite a cheering section. Her dad and I, his mother, and Celeste's godparents were all there to watch her swim. I am sure she felt pressure to win, but it came primarily from her desire to take home the coveted trophy.

I can remember the coach warming up the team before the last meet. They all had matching swim suits and team shirts. There was lots of laughing and giggling that kept everyone calm. It made my heart sing to seeing children this age having fun in a sports environment. The opportunity for socialization was a very important thing to me. I'll admit that I felt deep parental pride when my daughter won a race; but, I was more interested in the joy I could see in her face after a win. She would leap out of the pool and immediately start chattering with her friends. It was only later that we would learn that as you moved to higher levels in your chosen sport, "fun" was not necessarily part of the equation.

The final competition of the summer began with very young children who were only five or six years old. Competition progressed through each age group. As the various swimmers from our team would do well, their parents congratulated one another and extended excited warm wishes to all the swimmers. We were a large "swim family," supporting each and every child who was brave enough to swim a tough race.

Finally, it was time for the twelve and thirteen year old girls to compete. Celeste's godmother had brought a gold charm that said, "#1." It was very thoughtful gift, but I asked, "What if she doesn't win?"

Her godmother said, "She will!"

The first event was the backstroke. Celeste and Andrea, her main competitor, were out in the lead well ahead of the four other swimmers in their heat. Andrea had a better turn at the wall and she beat Celeste by just a second at the finish line. Next, they swam against one another in the butterfly. This time, Celeste beat Andrea. The last rotation was the freestyle, Celeste's favorite event. She flew off the blocks, nailed the flip-turn at the wall, and beat Andrea by quite a margin. Success! She had been the winner in two of the three events. The coveted trophy was hers!

Andrea shook Celeste's hand when she knew she was not going to be the winner that summer. It was a real mark of class and good sportsmanship; but, it was the last time I saw this sort of thing as Celeste moved into more demanding training in the pool. The two girls would meet again down the road under different circumstances, but I was pleased at the display of sportsmanship shown by each young woman that day. They both demonstrated a "let the best woman win" attitude and were able to remain friends during the years ahead.

After all the races were completed, the award winners were announced for each age group. Once again the winners heard their names called over the public address system as they received their trophies. As a proud mother, I wiggled my way through the crowd to see Celeste claim her prize from the meet director. I got a great picture of her shaking his hand while she firmly grasped her award in her other hand.

All of the friends and relatives who had come to watch Celeste were thrilled for her. Her godmother presented her with the "#1" charm and I loaned her my gold necklace so she could put the charm on and wear it. As we all left for breakfast, we were both excited and relieved that the pressure was over. Celeste ate like a hungry truck driver as she shot glances at the trophy sitting proudly on the table. It was an exciting ending to another season spent in the pool, doing what she loved to do.

That year, we had planned our summer vacation around the swim season. We knew Celeste was particularly important to her team as a relay "finisher." Her sport was still new to us and we were pleased to accommodate. We had planned to leave town just days after her big win, but another mother from the team begged us to stay for the team banquet. She was reluctant to say why, and I was confused. We acquiesced, and attended the banquet with all of the swimmers who had participated during the summer. There were awards given for Most Improved Swimmer, Best Attendance, and other successes. Then, to my surprise, came the "Most Valuable Boy" and "Most Valuable Girl" (MVP) trophies. The boy was announced first. I had a feeling that Celeste might be a contender,

## Chapter 3: Success in the Pool

but didn't want to get too excited. Finally, it came time for the Most Valuable Girl award. All of our eyes were glued on her coach who would make the presentation. With a smile, and a glance in our direction, we heard her coach announce her name! I felt deep parental pride as I watched her coach present her with the Most Valuable Girl Swimmer award. After receiving the trophy, Celeste walked over to where I was sitting and handed her prize to me! The message was clear: "Thank you Mom, for believing in me, supporting me and helping me achieve this goal." I put on my sunglasses so that no one could see the tears beginning to cloud my eyes.

Since we had delayed our summer trip, I made an appointment to see the head coach before we left. We were not certain of the next step for Celeste in the world of swimming and wanted his opinion. Celeste had achieved the highest honors in league swimming and would be too old to participate the following year. All of us needed some professional advice on how to proceed, as well as what to do the following summer. Her coach's advice stunned me. I spent the next two vacation weeks pondering his words. Although I was excited at what he said, I knew it would require an even greater commitment from all of us. Furthermore, I didn't want to push Celeste too hard.

Our family decision that summer was destined to impact us in ways we didn't understand at that time. Looking back, that season was a time of dynamic change for all three of us. It would be many years, and many tears, before we would recover from the dark and negative side of sports which can happen when there is poor leadership, combined with unethical coaches, parents and swimmers. Our descent into a dark and lonely world, known only by other elite athletes, was about to begin. It was time to "buckle our seatbelts."

Chapter Four

# Moving Up in the World of Swimming

T HE WORDS FROM CELESTE'S summer coach kept running through my mind as we were enjoying our summer vacation. I kept hearing him say, "Celeste is a gifted swimmer. With proper coaching, there is still time for her to excel in national level swimming. She has everything it takes to get to the Olympics…if she has the drive to do so."

The Olympics? My daughter? I was feeling both pride and fear at the same time. Two important questions ran through my mind: Did we have the dedication to become full-time swim parents…driving for hours, every day, to-and-from a private swim club? And, did Celeste even want to do that?

We discussed our next step a lot during our two-week vacation. Celeste was seemingly secure with the thought that even though she might be winning many of the races, she would still have friends and enjoy a social life. That is what she had experienced so far and that is what she was expecting to continue. So was I.

When we returned from our summer vacation, Celeste began the eighth grade. She decided she wanted to try "Fall League" swimming. That meant a more difficult daily work out with a "private club" for three months in the autumn. We had just such a club in our suburban city. As one might expect, the private club came with monthly dues, and the need for more equipment like swimsuits, caps and goggles. It was going to take a lot of time and money to continue supporting her in this sport. As far as Ben was concerned, he was at peace with the expenditures. His family had supported him as a teen while he was making himself known as a talented shooter.

Celeste had to "try out" before she could join the private swim club: there were no mediocre swimmers at this new level of competition. The club swimmers were the best in the city and many of them had won other Summer League Championships just like Celeste. Some swimmers and their families drove from other parts of the state to be part of the new club. It didn't take long to understand that Celeste was now a small fish in a very big pond.

The coach who watched her tryout placed her with other swimmers her age. They worked out at a junior high pool fairly close to our home. The practices were after

## Chapter 4: Moving Up in the World of Swimming

school each day during the evening hours. I can remember the first practice session clearly. The coach seemed stern and demanding. When I introduced the two of us, he never smiled as he crisply told Celeste to go get in the pool. Period. There was no more laughing and giggling among the swimmers; this was serious business.

I also had yet to understand that for some parents winning was everything; they were driven and determined that their children would get to the top. After all, college scholarships and money from sponsors were available for those who made it to the Senior National level, (the Olympic Trials). In spite of all the differences I was observing, I was still a very naïve mom thinking this would be "fun" for my child.

Celeste worked hard while I tried to keep it easy and enjoyable for her. Conversely, her two coaches barked orders at our children in the pool, insisting that they carry out their instruction perfectly. I worried about the pressure that Celeste might be feeling, but she didn't want to quit. She practiced hard and performed well at the fall meets. She didn't win every race, but that was an important lesson. It wasn't long before she found out that no matter how talented you are, there was always another swimmer who could beat you.

After the Fall League, there was a natural progression into full-time, year-round swimming. We were on our way to discovering what happens as you make your way up the ladder to an elite level in any sport. The swim meets were now "sanctioned" and governed by the United States Swimming Association. Our daughter was now a registered athlete who had a number. It was rather like a Social Security number in the world of swimming. All of her official times were logged in a national registry at the end of each meet. In order for the times to be recorded accurately, the finish line at every pool had a "touch pad" swimmers needed to touch in order to automatically record their times. Their times were displayed on a large electronic score board that all could see. In addition to this device, parents were expected to time the swimmers in case of an electronic malfunction. Every meet involved a cadre of persons monitoring computers and calculating statistics as official times were printed and posted. There were a number of disqualifying judges dressed in white who made certain that the starts were legal and no official rules were broken. At age thirteen, Celeste found herself competing with the best from other private clubs from all over the Western United States. Along with this came more and more pressure to win!

 Her dad and I had never made an issue of winning. Nevertheless, the pressure of winning came from a multitude of other sources. Even at this level, winning becomes an institutional objective. It is not only the individual who benefits from winning, but it is also the coaches, the team, the school, the parents, the city and even the state. This occurs because the coaches and the schools are judged by the performance of their swimmers and how they are ranked. Since many parents wanted their children to excel with the hope of a college scholarship, I was quickly beginning to experience the-so-called "Little League" mentality; angry parents confronting coaches and judges, as well as coaches berating the children for mistakes made in the pool. I was only there to support my child no matter how she performed and this behavior seemed foreign to me. It simply didn't occur to me to be cross with the coaches or to challenge a call made by a disqualifying judge.

Celeste was required to train once a day for two hours in the evening. The drive to and from the pool was forty minutes, so that left little time for homework and dinner. This was an adjustment for our family because "dinner together" had been enforced from the time Celeste was a small child.

At this level of competition, swim practice took place in the cold and rain of the winter months. The pools were heated, but getting in and out was painful! As Celeste got older, she was required to train both before and after school, spending at least four hours in the pool each day. In addition to this, there was a trip to the gym twice a week for weight training. During the summer months, the training was even more rigorous and demanding, but we followed along, still doing what was expected.

Looking back, I am sure I was perceived as a "loner" by many of the swimmers' parents; a quiet mom who kept to herself while watching her child swim. I used the time to read books or do needle work, unlike most of the other parents who seemed to thrive on gossip and parking-lot politics. Since her dad was still involved in the shooting sports, he was rarely available for the afternoon drive to and from the pool. That job fell to me. As a result, Celeste and I made the trip Monday through

Saturday every week. However, it wasn't that simple. We were quick to discover that official swim meets lasted for three days; Friday evening, all day Saturday, and all day Sunday. When swimmers were fast enough during the morning sessions and made the finals, they were required to come BACK in the evening for more competition. As you might guess, Celeste always made the finals and was expected to be back for the evening relays.

There was always a meet somewhere in the state at least twice a month. When Celeste's team was competing, it was assumed that she would be there. Being absent was not an option. She was a top swimmer, and her coaches demanded her best efforts. As her mother, I was beginning to become resentful that my daughter was swimming so many races, as well as being placed as the anchor on relays. It seemed as if she was swimming twice as hard as the other swimmers and she was only thirteen years old. I asked myself, "Why does this fall to Celeste alone?" Yes, she was gifted, but I began to sense a level of abuse going on as I slowly became aware of how the "system" worked. I wasn't happy about it at all. Still, my "mantra" was to keep quiet and not interfere. I didn't want to be "tagged" as a difficult parent, so I stayed out of the way and continued to support my daughter.

On one particularly cold weekend, close to Christmas during her eighth-grade year, I was sitting just behind the starting blocks in the role of parent timer. Celeste had swum several races, but one of her coaches found fault with something she had done. Not realizing that I was sitting close by, he chose to berate my child harshly in front of her teammates and me. I could see the look of pain on her face and her determination to remain unfazed. I'll admit that he was an "equal opportunity" abuser, meaning he treated most of the kids harshly; however, I was shocked at what I heard him say to her. Shocked and angry! Because of my background in teaching, I knew that negative motivation does not work with most children, especially girls. Boys are socialized to be "tough" from the time they are born; but, teen-aged girls needed to be handled differently. I "simmered" for awhile, pondering what to do about the verbal assaults being hurled at my daughter.

Later in the day, I saw the offending coach standing alone. The head coach was not there that day or I would have approached him with my concerns. Going against my own personal "rules" about parental interference, I walked up to the assistant coach and asked, "Is Celeste on your list today?"

He looked confused. "What list?"

"Your shit list," said the quiet little mother who normally stayed out of this kind of confrontation.

I went on to say that thirteen year old girls are very sensitive to criticism and do not respond well to the kind of harsh remarks he was doling out regularly. He looked a bit guilty but never apologized. My message seemed to have fallen on deaf ears.

After witnessing this kind of "put-down" time after time for nearly a year, I decided to write a letter to the head coach. Because he worked with older swimmers, and had developed a professional style of coaching, I felt he really needed to know about the unprofessional behavior exhibited by some of his other coaches. I wrote him a very detailed and heartfelt letter. I also sent a copy of the letter to the president of the parents' group. I expected some kind of comment or response from someone, but heard nothing. I was beginning to see a lack of strong leadership and I wondered who was truly in charge of this swim program. I also wondered about the loyalty, or lack of loyalty, of the staff toward the man who was being paid to run the program. As I watched the behavior of coaches and swimmers alike, I began to have serious doubts regarding our decision to pursue club swimming. With this concern in mind, I started studying other teams when we attended different meets during the year. I found what appeared to be the same stern, uncaring behavior toward the swimmers. It was as if it were an Olympic competition and not a local meet between teenage children.

As Celeste moved through the summer and into the ninth grade, the situation became more complex. She began to swim for her high school, even though she was attending a junior high campus. As a family, this move required more sacrifice in terms of time, money and effort. Since Celeste was required to not only train with her high school team, but her club team as well, I became the quintessential "swim mom" driving my child to two practices each day. I wondered how she could continue to do well in school and spend so much time in the swimming pool. The bottom line was that Celeste still wanted to swim, and we, as parents, chose to continue supporting her efforts.

# Chapter Five
# The 5A Championships

THE FALL SEASON OF her ninth-grade year required a huge adjustment from Celeste. She was not only swimming as a member of her high school team, but was also continuing to train with her club team as well. The high school swim coach required Celeste to train at least two days a week with the high school group, but allowed her four days to train with her club team. This required her to be in the pool before and after school, six days a week. In addition, her club team required participation in club meets on weekends, and her high school had "after school" meets against other high schools at least every two weeks. If this weren't enough, Celeste was adjusting to the scholastic requirements of the ninth grade. It was quite a shock going from junior high courses to the rigors of a more demanding high school curriculum.

The driving time required for this routine was substantial. Not only was I providing transportation for my daughter, I found myself driving other people's children to and from the pool because most parents worked during the day. I had made a commitment to my daughter, and I was lucky to have a working husband who supported my decision. My work as a substitute teacher fell by the wayside as I concentrated on keeping our family together as a unit, running a household, and taking care of our several household pets.

The fact that I only had one child gave me the freedom to attend all of her meets and support her athletic lifestyle. Mothers and fathers with more than one child had to alternate between the activities of their children, not having the luxury of attending all of their swim meets. There were, however, some parents who NEVER attended meets. They simply didn't take the time to do so. They had large families and just sent their children to swim without supporting them at practice or at their meets. This was very hard for me to understand because I took my role as a mother very seriously. My thinking was that I only had one chance to "mother" properly and I was going to give it everything I had. As a teacher, I had learned that the quantity and quality of time you invest is directly related to the success and productivity of your children as adults.

I am proud to say that I never missed one of Celeste's meets. She could always check the stands and find me there as she stepped up on the starting blocks. I was a security blanket of sorts, and it became more important to her as her situation went from joyous, to a decline into a world of fear and darkness.

As of now, Celeste's high school coach was very pleased to have such a talented freshman on the team. Celeste was able help her team win nearly every meet that they attended that fall. After meet days, I would buy a local paper to view the final results. I eagerly clipped out articles about her team. Most of the time I would find my daughter's name listed as "winner" in several events. Yes, I was a very proud parent.

There were several other stand-out swimmers on her team, but Celeste gained considerable visibility as she won her freestyle events and anchored winning relays. Much of the attention she received was due to the fact that she was small in stature. This made it even more exciting to see the "half-pint" barrel into the finish line and win a race. I could see the look of genuine awe on people's faces as they watched her swim. Parents would often stop me and tell me how much they enjoyed watching her swim to a win.

Still, I was beginning to sense unrest among the parents and swimmers who were not getting the attention being given to my daughter. She and I were embarrassed at all the fuss, and hoped that it would subside. The coaches tried their best to NOT show favoritism, but that was hard to do when you had a gifted athlete on the team. I was noticing more and more grumbling in and around the pool: parents were asking, "Why isn't my child chosen as the anchor, or put in the fastest heats?"

These kinds of questions were coming primarily from parents with a "Little League" mentality; by this I mean "the parents are right and the coaches are wrong." It was, however, only a matter of time until Celeste could beat them all in her specific events. This seemed fair to me, but not to a number of other overly involved families. My mantra was still, "Let the coaches do their jobs while I stay out of the way."

Meanwhile, Celeste's club coaches were pressuring her to make her Junior National times. Junior National qualifying times would allow her to travel to large out-of-town meets where only the finest swimmers in the nation competed. Up to now, Celeste had managed the pressure well. She was keeping her grades up in school while enjoying winning with a focus on improving her times.

When it came time for the All City Championships, where the best city high school swimmers would compete, Celeste was chosen to swim the 50 and 100 freestyle events. My beloved aunt came over from California to watch her grand-niece in the pool. As a teen-ager, she had watched her brother (my father) become Los Angeles City Champion in the same swimming events! She was excited to see her grand-niece, two generations younger, accomplish the same goal. We all had our cameras ready to capture the first big event of her first high school swim season.

As Celeste climbed up on the blocks before the 50 freestyle, she did her usual "check" for mom. This time she found both me and her great-aunt standing on the sidelines. The starting gun went off and she sliced

## Chapter 5: The 5A Championships

cleanly into the water. Much to our delight she touched the wall first! She had beaten seven other top swimmers from around the city. As I looked at my aunt, a normally stoic and pulled-together lady, I saw tears running down her face. She exclaimed, "Oh, Leslie, she is just like Tommy!" (my dad).

Celeste's high school coach was obviously pleased with her performance as he anticipated the great things that could happen during the upcoming State Championships – the 5A Finals.

As the meet we were attending continued, it was now time for Celeste to swim the 100 freestyle event. Once again she smoothly moved through the water, touched the wall first and won the race. Unknown to me at the time, one kind father video taped all of Celeste's races. When the winners were announced, he taped that too! I was indeed grateful and I still have those images to this day.

At the awards ceremony, the winners' names came blaring over the loudspeakers. There was lots of cheering as the swimmers took their places for first, second, and third on the winner's blocks for each event. It was a proud moment to see Celeste stand on the top block as she received each of her awards. One of the men's service clubs had sponsored the meet and gave specially engraved towels to each of the winners in addition to their trophies. Since Celeste had won two beautiful towels, she gave one to her high school coach. This was definitely a "photo opportunity" so I photographed the two of them together, holding the coveted towels and smiling broadly.

The final event of the high school swim season was held at a large university, two hours from home. It was November, and the finest swimmers from all over the state would be there competing in the 5A Championships. The competing high schools were placed into divisions according to the high schools' student population. Celeste's high school was large, as were all the other schools in the 5A Division. This meant that there would be more swimmers with faster times. Celeste knew that the competition would be fierce, but she looked forward to the challenge. There were still some swimmers she had never met; swimmers from around the state that she would be competing against for the first time.

Celeste had always accompanied me as we drove to the meets; this time Celeste traveled with her team via a van driven by her coach and assistant coach. This was a major adjustment for me: I felt completely alone as I began a two hour drive to the university where the meet was scheduled. I had no clue where to park and no idea where the pool was situated on this very large campus. Ben was at work, so he was unable to attend. I set out alone because I was determined to do so.

All of the swimmers spent one night near the university and had to be prepared to swim the next day. After my two hour drive that started five o'clock in the morning, I arrived in time to see them warming up in the pool. The covered grandstand was filled with hundreds of spectators. Swimmers were all over the place, talking, laughing, and throwing water on each other, as they waited for their turn to warm up in the pool. I managed to find a tiny spot for my "mom" chair.

At this big event, parents were not allowed on the swim deck itself. Since I wanted Celeste to know I was there, I stood at a rail surrounding the pool and waited for her to start looking for me. When she finally found me I could see a look of relief and happiness on her face. That was something that had never changed over the eleven years she was involved with swimming: My daughter wanted me at her races throughout her swimming "career." Some of the swimmers told their parents to stay home! I feel the reason she wanted me there is because I never put pressure on her, and I was always smiling at the end of a race no matter how she performed.

I had no idea how Celeste would perform at the championships with so many swimmers, coaches, and parents in attendance. It was a huge event, with the fastest swimmers from grades nine through twelve from all over the state. Celeste's individual events would be the 50 and 100 freestyle, in addition to her participation on all the relays. She was only a freshman and she was competing against seniors.

A few moments before she stepped up on the starting blocks for the 50 freestyle, I made my way through the throng of parents and found a place at the rail. On the outside I seemed composed, but inside I was nervous for my daughter. The gun went off and I could tell she had a perfect start. The start is crucial in the 50 freestyle because it involves only one lap of the pool. It's known to be a real "horse race" where hundredths of seconds can determine the winner. The "wave" of swimmers moved toward the finish line. Celeste was swimming in lane five. When all of the swimmers reached the wall, the times flashed up on the score board. She was second; the winner had beaten her by two one-hundredths of a second. A huge roar came from the Painted Mountain parent group! Celeste, the little freshman from Painted Mountain High School, had achieved a huge success. A big smile lit up my face as I waved at my daughter who found me in the crowd. I quietly returned to my chair, trying my best to stay composed.

A little later it was time for her to swim the 100 freestyle. Once again, I wormed my way to the rail to watch her swim. She had a good start, and made good turns, but the six-foot girls were able to out-reach her as they touched the wall. She placed fourth, but did achieve a personal best time. I looked over to see the same dad video taping my daughter's race! I didn't own a video camera and I was grateful he was acting as the photographer.

Finally, Celeste was allowed to come join me in the grandstand area. She looked like a celebrity as she made her way through the crowd, reaching out to shake hands with parents from her team. I tried not to beam, but when she got to me, she got a big bear hug and a kiss. It was a proud moment, indeed. My freshman had made herself known at the High School State Swimming Championships at age fourteen.

As the day came to a close, most of the swimmers went home with their parents or coaches. Even though it was getting late, and I had a two hour drive home in the dark, I was not about to miss the awards ceremony where Celeste would receive two medals for her performances that day. I proudly took pictures of my daughter as she was called to the Olympic-style award blocks for the 50 and the 100 freestyle events. The medals were placed around her neck, Olympic-style. The only thing missing was the National Anthem!

Celeste chose to ride home with a friend and her parents. Finding myself driving alone again, I wondered how I would manage emotionally if she ever did make an Olympic team. The chances of that were slim; but, it was fun just dreaming about it.

Chapter Six

# The Letterman's Jacket

THE HIGH SCHOOL SWIMMING SEASON was officially over after the State Championships. What remained was the team banquet that honored all of the team swimmers; even those who did not get to participate in the finals. The banquet turned out to be a casual evening held in the Painted Mountain High School cafeteria. After the coaches made a few comments during dinner, it was time for the awards ceremony.

There were several outstanding girls and boys on the high school team and only the coaches knew who had earned the most overall points for the team. Celeste was only a freshman, so I expected the awards to go to older swimmers. One older girl I felt sure would win the Most Valuable Girl award was a female swimmer who had achieved a Junior National time in the breast stroke.

As the winners were announced, the Most Valuable Boy trophy went to a young man who was a junior. We were pleased because he was one of Celeste's teammates in USS club swimming so we knew him and his parents well. It was this young man's father who had video taped all of Celeste's races.

When it came time for the Most Valuable Girl Award, the coach spoke well of the winner and noted her many accomplishments. I remember holding my breath for what seemed an eternity before he announced the winner's name. It was Celeste! A big smile lit up her face as she left her spot by her friends, walked up to the coach, and accepted the award with a handshake. I was very excited, but tried to remain calm and collected. Celeste looked my way to see my reaction. She knew that I was very proud, even though I may have looked "casual" about the whole thing. This had always been my style. I had a great "poker" face and I used it when I didn't want anyone to know how I really felt. "Let 'em guess," was my attitude.

I looked around the room and studied the faces of some of the faster swimmers who did not win. They looked disgruntled and displeased with the coaches' decision to give the trophy to Celeste, a freshman. Their parents had the same unhappy expression. Only one man congratulated us about our child's win. He shook Celeste's hand and said something kind to the both of us. I was definitely uncomfortable with the lack of good sportsmanship being demonstrated. The negative attitude that seemed tied to this world of competition was still

## Chapter 6: The Letterman's Jacket

foreign to me. So much of everyone's behavior seemed petty and unprofessional. I was thinking, "What is the matter with these people? This is a team; why aren't they happy for one of their winning team members?"

In contrast, there didn't seem to be any negativism toward the young man who received the Most Valuable Boy award, just my daughter. I was still unwilling to believe that this apparent jealousy was aimed squarely at my child. I would have said something nice and congratulated the winner no matter who had won the trophy. It was becoming quite clear to me that my attitude seemed to be in the minority. Most of the other parents and swimmers apparently had a different mind set.

About a week after the awards banquet, the local sports shop let us know that Celeste's beautiful letterman's jacket was ready to be picked up. When my aunt had visited us during the City Championships, she insisted on ordering a jacket for Celeste knowing that was another large expenditure that was hard for us to manage. We were grateful to my generous aunt, and very excited when we picked up her new coat. It fit beautifully, creating another exciting mother-daughter moment. My daughter had "lettered" in swimming as a freshman!

She proudly wore her jacket to school where many of her teachers wanted to know how well she had performed. There was one instructor in particular, her chemistry teacher, who was proud of her athletic accomplishments as well as her performance in his class.

Celeste returned to her USS club team to continue swimming throughout the winter. She wore her letterman's jacket to meets, but found that this was generally met with reproach from her female teammates. For some reason, several of the girls had decided that they no longer cared to be Celeste's friends, even though they had known each other for years. Even worse, this behavior seemed to carry over into their time together during school. As a result, Celeste found herself being placed outside her group of disloyal "former" friends. She began spending her lunch hour in the school library reading, obviously avoiding the pain of seeing her former friends in the lunch room laughing and giggling without her.

During this period, Celeste's teachers chose her to become a member of the National Junior Honor Society. Again, this honor seemed to add to the angst she was feeling about being "thrown away" by her girlfriends. Not wanting to upset me, or have me worry, she did not let me know that she was spending more and more time in the library alone, reading and studying. When I found out about it, I did worry, and I wasn't sure what to do. I knew how girls her age often behaved; but, I felt powerless to change their bad behavior. I assumed that by the time they left the ninth grade, moving on to their sophomore year, their bad attitudes would disappear.

Sadly, since the letterman's jacket had become a point of contention at school and every meet, Celeste stopped wearing it, even during the coldest winter months. It just hung in the closet, unused. This "symbol" of success became a sad reminder that the girls whom she thought were her friends had turned their backs on her. She still sat with her team at the weekend meets, but the whole "feel" of the group was different. Gone were the days of laughter and fun with teammates her age. Instead, Celeste was becoming isolated, feeling alone on the kool deck as she awaited her turn on the blocks.

All of this angst wasn't directed at Celeste alone. The swimmers' parents also treated me with disdain and obvious exclusion. It mattered little to me how I was treated, but I was very upset about Celeste's situation. I didn't approach the head coach about this because I assumed he wouldn't understand the issues of teenage girls. I realize now that I should have spoken to him about this problem before it became any worse. At the time, I was still hoping that Celeste would work this out with her friends.

When some of my family and friends became aware of the overall situation, they wondered why I did not just pull Celeste out of the swim program. At the time I felt this would be the "easy" way out and we never seemed to do things the easy way. It didn't seem right to quit because of some unpleasant adolescent behavior. I continued to hope that they would all mature and eventually this problem would go away. I still had no idea how brutal young people could be to one another, but I was about to find out the hard way.

## Chapter Seven
# Bodyguard

CELESTE CONTINUED TO SWIM for her USS club team throughout the summer months before entering her sophomore year of high school. She put on a brave face, continued to win races and even improved her times. Unfortunately, most of the girls her age completely ignored her at meets. I encouraged her to befriend the younger swimmers by being a kind and caring "pal." She was always good with young kids and they loved being around her. Still, there seemed to be a dark cloud surrounding Celeste. This took the joy out of competition and attending the meets because it became painful for her. It appeared that Celeste's peer group had abandoned her!

Regardless, her coaches still counted on her in the pool, so we made our best effort to keep our emotionality in check. I found myself giving her pep talks before, during, and after the meets. In addition to my "mom" role, I had become her counselor as well. I knew that all good parents wear many different "hats" according to the situation at hand; for this reason I was doing a lot of behind-the-scenes coaching just to keep her interested in her sport. It was exhausting, but the two of us kept on participating. I had never been a "quitter" in my life and I wanted my child to have the same value system. Running away from conflict was not my style, and I wanted Celeste to know what "bravery in the face of challenge" was all about.

I remember clearly when the first sign of true bullying behavior became too obvious to ignore. I was sitting alone at a meet one afternoon, reading my book, waiting for Celeste to swim. She came up to me with a panicked look. I asked, "What is the matter?"

She said, "Mom! My towel is missing! It was lying on the ground beside me with all of my things on it, and it's gone!"

It was the towel she had won at the City Championships. It had special meaning to both of us. I quickly looked around the area to see if she might have put it somewhere close-by. So, there I was, looking around in the swimmers area, with the "annoyed" junior high set watching me. I could tell by the look on their faces that they were wondering, "What is SHE doing down here?"

I walked toward the starting blocks to see if the missing towel was there and found nothing. The next stop was to the locker room where I checked to see if someone had tossed it in there. I found no trace of Celeste's towel, knowing it was not like her to lose important keepsakes.

### Chapter 7: Bodyguard

I suspected it had been thrown away, but I was too proud to go "dumpster diving."

As time marched on that summer we had swim caps mysteriously disappear, goggles went missing and other swimming paraphernalia seemed to vanish into thin air. Celeste and I were both starting to look over our shoulders to see who might be waiting to "lift" more of our personal items. Even though I knew the group of suspected bullies was afraid of me, I kept a close eye on all of my things too. I would not have been surprised if they "filched" some of my things while I watched my daughter swim. As time continued, it became increasingly difficult for my daughter and me to even attend the meets, but both of us were determined to "keep on keeping on." Never did Celeste say to me, "Mom, I want to quit." She had my fighting spirit and I was proud of her attitude.

As time went on, she and I began to sit apart from the "others," while I became a guardian of both her things and her. I know this must have appeared odd to other families as they wondered why Celeste no longer sat with her team. I was afraid to say anything to anyone because I couldn't "prove" any of my suspicions. I had never caught any of the teens in the act of stealing. They were "stealth" stealers, taking belongings from a swimmer who could beat them in the pool. "Petty jealousy" was the name of the game and I was determined to win the game.

After the more important meets, the coaches would stay and collect any medals that their swimmers had earned since most of the families had already headed home. They had files for each swimmer and they would file the medals by name so that the swimmers could collect them later. Because of this procedure I knew when Celeste had medaled at a meet, and I assumed that the awards would be safe in her file folder until she could collect them.

When her medals started to disappear from the file, knowing she had not picked them up personally, I became enraged. This really was happening and I could not do anything about it. If I told on kids with bad attitudes, life would have become even more difficult for Celeste. So, I kept my silence. More and more I was becoming one angry mom who felt very alone in the world of club swimming.

As Celeste began her sophomore year, her high school swimming coach was more than happy to see her rejoining the team. I hoped that the high school swim season would help her regain her love of the sport. Even though the bullying swimmers swam on both the United States Swimming Club (USS club) and the high school teams, the high school team offered a more laid-back atmosphere because there were all levels of swimmers on the team. Regardless, Celeste was still training with her USS club team, and the "pack" of teen-aged girls kept after Celeste by tormenting her verbally and stealing her things. All I knew was that it was costing more and more to replace stolen things, and my vigil at every meet was becoming more intense. I was also beginning to "simmer." I had a long fuse, but I wasn't certain how long I could remain calm about this continuing harassment.

That fall, new students from other junior high schools joined the high school team. Celeste befriended one of the new swimmers who knew nothing about her. I even became friends with her mother while we passed the time at meets and watched our girls swim. I assumed it was only a matter of time before the usual "gossip" would be heard by my new "mom" friend, so I just enjoyed the friendship for whatever time we had left.

The bully "pack animals" quickly caught on to Celeste's new friendship. It wasn't long before they did everything they could to destroy the fun that Celeste was having with her new swimming friend. As it turned out, they were totally successful. It all began when the bully group starting having "sleepovers." They invited Celeste's friend to join in without inviting Celeste. This hurt Celeste knowing her new friend had decided to be "chummy" with the girls who were actively bullying her. I continued wearing my hat as counselor, trying to cheer my unhappy child.

During this difficult period, Celeste's father was working the "swing" shift. He went to work at 2:30 PM and left work at 11 PM. Because of his work schedule, he could not attend the meets and help me "guard" our daughter. Most of what he knew about the situation was gleaned through what Celeste and I shared with him. He was good emotional support for both of us, but could not physically be there to help diffuse the situation. I firmly believe that if there had been a stronger "Dad presence," the bullying would not have escalated to the point that it did.

The bullying reached one of its high points one Saturday night in October. Celeste and I were home alone watching a movie. After we went to bed around 10 PM, I was awakened an hour later by Ben when he arrived home from work. He said, "Have you seen our yard?"

I asked, "What is the matter with our yard?"

I quickly pulled on some clothes and went out to find toilet paper strung all over the plants and trees. Not only that, but a mother lode of trash had been tossed right in the middle of our yard. I felt the blood rush to my head in a hot flash of anger! I knew exactly who had made this terrible mess. Ben said, "I saw all of them. When I turned into the driveway, they jumped into a van and roared off!"

I asked, "Was it who I think it was?"

"Yes." he replied.

Frustrated, I blurted, "Why didn't you grab your shotgun and let them hear you rack it?"

At this point my angst got the best of me. I said, "Ben, this is not just a teenage prank. We are being harassed and this has got to stop."

He agreed, but we did not have a concrete plan as to how we might stop this problem that was quickly spinning out of control. In the darkness of my sleepless night, I thought to myself, "Ok, this time it was toilet paper and garbage. What will it be next time?" I was sure there would be a next time.

When Celeste arrived at school the following Monday, she confronted her new swimming friend. "Were you at my house on Saturday night, riding in a van?"

"Yes," she answered.

Once again Celeste had been betrayed by another girl "posing" as a friend. She was heartbroken.

That week, the high school coach scheduled a meeting after practice. I was concerned about Celeste's emotional state, knowing that she felt she was at practice with "traitors," if you will. I arrived early to pick her up from the meeting. As I sat waiting in my car she burst out of the locker room door with tears in her eyes. With a look of panic on her face she said, "Mother! Hire a lawyer and get me out of here!"

That was it! My fuse had burned to its end. The "bomb" who was "Mom" was about to go off. I said to Celeste, "Stay in the car, with the doors locked. I am going to talk to your coach."

She didn't tell me no. She knew it was past time for me to get involved.

I waited until I found the head coach alone. We had always had a pleasant rapport, but he could tell by my expression that something was very wrong. I asked, "What just happened in your team meeting?"

Her coach looked confused, and said: "I don't know, but Celeste was very quiet and looked upset."

I said, "Celeste just got into the car in tears because of derogatory remarks aimed at her. Let me tell you what has been going on for the last year. A particular group of girls on this team, and on Celeste's USS club team, have been bullying her for over a year. I have had it. I know you are probably not aware of this, but the bullying has snowballed into a huge problem. They have stolen from her, belittled her, lied about her, started rumors about our family, and this has got to stop. I realize I am hitting you hard with this information, but you need to know this about some of your swimmers."

I then named each and every one of them. My parting words were, "I expect you to help me put a stop to this behavior now." I left her coach with a stunned look on his face.

I wasn't finished. I called Ben and told him what I was going to do next. My next stop was to her USS club swimming group. Normally, Celeste would have gone to club practice, but I had her wait in the car with the doors locked. I found the head coach and pulled him aside. When I finished with my tirade, he was just as stunned as the high school coach had been. He could not believe this was going on. He said he had never seen this kind of hate in all his years of coaching swimming. "Leslie," he asked, "Why didn't you tell me this before now?"

I answered, "What could you have done? You couldn't stand guard over the team files and Celeste's towels and belongings; further, you could not have stopped all of the gossip, lies and harassment that has been directed toward her. These kids are 'pack animals.' They are only fierce in a group. One-on-one they are weak, but this group of girls has been tormenting my daughter for over a year and it has escalated to an unacceptable level. I am this close to pulling Celeste out of swimming altogether. I want you to know who is responsible because these kids are on your team. They are bullies, and this mom has had enough."

He stood looking at me speechless. I saw a look of sadness in his eyes as I marched off the deck. All the while, Celeste's teammates had ceased swimming and had watched the angry mom on deck talking with their coach. I felt sure they had heard some of my impassioned comments. Knowing well that the "word" would spread rapidly, I had no trouble imagining what their comments might be, "Celeste's mom went postal at the pool!" More gossip for the gossip mill, but I didn't care.

My next stop was at the home of a member of the team's board of directors. This was a particularly poignant meeting because this man had always been kind to Celeste, as well as one of her biggest supporters. I was about to let him know that his daughter was one of Celeste's tormenters. She was the one Celeste's father saw driving the van the night of the swimming "invasion" at our home. She was sixteen, while the rest of the "pack" was only fifteen.

I knocked on his door. As the door opened, I saw his panicked daughter scurry to the back of the house. He looked confused as I asked, "May I come in?"

Celeste was still in the locked car. I don't know who I thought was going to "get" her, but my adrenaline was running full force not wanting to take any chances with her safety. I sat on his couch, looked him straight in the eye, and with great control I slowly said, "You are a member of the Board of Directors. You need to know that my daughter Celeste has been harassed and bullied for over a year. More importantly, you need to know that your own daughter has been involved. Saturday night, your daughter, and a car full of teens, decided to spread toilet paper all over our front yard. Not only that, they dumped a full can of trash in the middle of our yard. My husband saw them as he returned from work. It was your van they were driving, and I expect you to speak with your daughter. I don't want her or her friends near my home or my child ever again." I left him just as astonished as the other two adults with whom I had spoken.

My last "call" of the evening was the most difficult one. It was to the house of the main bully herself. She was the "ring leader" and I wanted to talk to her parents face to face. As I marched to the door, I felt something drop on my head from a second story window. It was damp and felt like spit! It didn't slow me down. I knocked on the door and "Madam Bully" answered. I asked, "Are your parents home?"

"No," she answered.

"May I come in? I'll wait," was my reply.

"We can't let anyone into the house when our parents aren't home."

It appeared that she was home alone with a younger brother. I continued. "Alright. I will speak to you from here. My message is for you. I know exactly what you and your gang of friends have been doing and I want it stopped. This has been going on for over a year, and I don't appreciate the stolen items, verbal harassment, disparaging remarks, and downright lies you and your friends have spread about Celeste and our family. All of the coaches and parents know who you are because you got caught last Saturday night at our house by Celeste's dad. I want this stopped now or I will report all of you to the police. And, let me add one more thing; if you bother my daughter ever again, even if Celeste catches a cold, I am going to blame it on you!"

At this point, I had my index finger in the face of this teen. I was enraged! She was a six-footer that put me up on my toes, waving my index finger wildly. She just stood there with a poker face. No fear. I couldn't believe it! I am a rather "soft spoken" woman, but when I am mad, get out of my way. Unlike the others, she had no visible reaction as she slowly closed the door.

On Thursday afternoon, the high school team had another meet at their practice pool. As I had expected, the gossip had reached epic proportions. The swimmers were still excluding my daughter so she sat by me until it was time to swim. I later learned that the parents, teachers, and coaches had heard that Mrs. Wood (me) was considering pulling her daughter out of swimming entirely.

As one of the races was about to begin, I saw some of the swimmers corner my child on the deck in a threatening manner as she got up to swim a race. I was seated in my portable chair watching it all happen. It seemed like a high-drama movie, but it was real. During the meet, I even had parents approach me as I was seated in my chair, challenging the possibility that I might remove Celeste from the team. I simply smiled, and told them it was none of their business what I "might" do.

The head coach was tense and barely looked at me. At one point, the high school Director of Athletics unexpectedly showed up to pay a visit to my chair. I felt like I was sitting in the electric chair, with the "current of discontent" full on. I knew exactly why the director had been sent to speak with me. We had never met, but he knew where I was seated. We talked for awhile, and although he tried to be kind, he let me know that he was very nervous about any plan to remove their "star" swimmer from the finals that were just around the corner. It was generally known that the 5A Championships rested squarely on the shoulders of my child. The parents were enraged at the thought of losing her and the coaches were frantic. Celeste noticed all of the activity taking place where I sat. She came over to me and exclaimed, "Mom! It looks like you are being attacked!"

I said, "Yes, but don't worry about me; I am doing fine. Just swim your best and let's get out of here and go home." I was worried about her and she was worried about me. We were quite a pair, my child and I.

Not only did Celeste do her best swimming that meet, her times were so good that they would have qualified her for the Junior National Championships in the 50 freestyle. Because it was not a sanctioned United States swim meet, the time didn't matter to anyone but me. I had witnessed my daughter swimming the race of her life; yet, it was a bittersweet moment. She was so angry, frustrated and full of adrenaline that she finished the race half a body length ahead of the other swimmers. This is unheard of in a 50 freestyle "horserace." As fate would have it, the parent-timer was one of the bully's mothers. For some reason, the time was never officially recorded. As a result,

## Chapter 7: Bodyguard

Celeste's outstanding performance was never entered into the official school records and was not reported in the morning papers along with other swimmer's times. I can only believe that it was a purposeful omission.

Once again, I felt sure that my "grace under fire" had calmed everything down at the swimming pool. I was proud of myself because I had remained serene and in charge, allowing others to appear as out of control.

The next day, Ben had the day off. I filled him in regarding the events of the last two days. I was feeling almost celebratory, thinking that Celeste and I had shown them all that we were strong and in control of the situation. It was another proud moment, but that moment did not last long.

About 1 PM on Friday afternoon, the phone rang. Celeste was on the other end of the line. Those were the days before cell phones, so I knew she must be calling from a pay phone somewhere. She said, in a hushed voice: "Mom, I am in danger. I'm hiding out here at school. It's not even safe for me to be here. One of the girls on the team (one of the bullies) is dating a gang member. She told me there was a 'hit' on my life if I dropped off the team. Please, come and get me; I am afraid someone may try to kill me!"

Without thinking twice I said, "Go to the library and stay where the librarian can see you. Try to look busy and wait there until I come and get you. I'll be there in ten minutes."

I felt weak and sick at my stomach. My knees buckled under me as I found a chair. I thought, "Surely, this can not really be happening." I felt like it was all a dream! But I knew Celeste well and I knew she was telling me the harsh truth.

My first thought after receiving the phone call was to get Celeste's father involved. However, because Ben had not been seen around the pool very often, I felt he would be of little help in dealing with the high school leadership. I walked back to Ben's home office and said, "There is an emergency at school. Celeste is fine at the moment, but she is in real danger. I am going to get her out of there right now."

On my way to the high school I thought about my options. There was only one clear answer. I was going to do what I needed to do and do it quickly. As far as I knew, my child's life was on the line. For the first time, I was truly afraid and I didn't feel strong at all.

## Chapter Eight

# Prison Break

As promised, I arrived at her high school in ten minutes and got permission to go "search" for my frightened daughter. Instead of finding her hiding in the library, I found her in tears, alone in the main hall. I asked her what had happened. Through teary eyes she said she had just attended a meeting and it had not gone well at all. She promised to tell me the story later. I said, "Come with me. I have made up my mind what we are going to do about this situation."

She looked hopeful, but skeptical at the same time. We went back out to the school secretary's desk. Without any opening comment I said, "I am removing my daughter from Painted Mountain High School. Now!"

It was the middle of fifth period and the secretary looked confused. I was beginning to become familiar with this "deer in the headlights" look from almost every adult I had encountered of late. She asked, "May I ask why?"

I said, "It is much too complicated to explain right now and it is personal in nature. Just tell me what I need to do to get my child out of this school."

Still somewhat startled she said, "Well, first, your daughter needs to turn in all of her books."

I said, "Fine. But I am going to go with her to wherever they happen to be."

The secretary appeared even more confused, but I felt no need to explain anything to her. I looked at Celeste and said quietly, "Take me with you to your locker, and anywhere else you have books or personal items. We need to get out of here."

By now Celeste had stopped crying. We hurried off to her locker mindful of anything or anyone who might try to harm her. I had no way of knowing if the story about the "hit" on her life was true or not; but, I was not going to take any chances. I felt like a Secret Service agent in some action film; I was ready to protect my child by literally "taking the bullet" if someone took a shot at her. Sadly, there had been weapons offenses at her high school that fall, and the thought had crossed my mind more than once that the "hit rumor" might be true.

We carefully went through her locker, locating her personal things and gathering up books and papers. She stuffed everything into her backpack as we quickly returned to the secretary's desk. Celeste gave the secretary her books, and without saying a thing I signed all of the paperwork that would release my daughter from her high school. I then asked to speak to the Director of Athletics. I wanted him to know, and to understand, what we were doing and why we were doing it.

The secretary said he was on the phone but would be out in a minute. We sat in the front office, feeling like we were in a timeless void. The director finally came out to greet us with a pleasant smile on his face. His smile quickly faded when he saw the stern look on my face. He invited me into his office and asked if he could speak to me privately. I was not happy about leaving Celeste in the lobby, but I felt she would be safe under the scrutiny of the nosy receptionist.

Upon entering the director's office, I found an empty chair. Unfortunately, I could no longer control my emotions as I started to explain what I was planning to do to him, the swim team and the high school. Here I was, pulling their top swimmer out of school just a week before the high school 5A finals. Celeste had set records there and I knew the he would not be happy about losing her. I had managed to stay "dry-eyed" for months, and was determined not to let anyone see my tears; but, I lost the "battle" that afternoon. I quickly put my sunglasses on so that the flood of tears would not be so obvious. It was a silly gesture because the wad of kleenexes in my hand, and my nose blowing, completely gave me away!

I explained the situation frankly and honestly. He looked angry at first, but when I expressed genuine concern for my child's safety, and when he realized that he could not ensure my daughter's safety, his facial expression changed. I felt sure he was a father with children of his own. Finally, he admitted that he would make the same choice if he was faced with our problem. Knowing our conversation was at a close, I stood up and shook his hand as he wished me the best of luck. I nodded through blinding tears as we left his office. I said nothing to the secretary as Celeste and I moved past her desk headed for home. I was a little "wobbly" on the stairs leading to the parking lot, but Celeste had a good grip on my arm. She hadn't seen her strong mom in tears too often and she was rightfully concerned.

We hurried to the car, looking behind us all the way. After locking the doors I said, "I had better 'dry up' or I can't drive us home safely."

I forced back the tears and concentrated on responsible driving. I felt a sense of comfort when I saw a peaceful look on Celeste's face as we drove home. I thought to myself, "She finally feels safe!" Her mom had pulled her out of a potentially dangerous situation and she looked grateful. It was a small, sweet moment to treasure in the midst of all the fear, frustration, and embarrassment we had just experienced.

I refused to let worry enter my mind about what we were going to do next. For the last time, we headed out of the school parking lot toward the safety of our home. I could see her old high school slowly disappear in my rear-view mirror. For just a moment I felt like we were making a "prison break". We were literally two fugitives running for our lives.

## Chapter Nine
# Angelic Surprise

B<small>Y THE TIME WE ARRIVED HOME</small> Ben was waiting. He wanted to hear all of the details about what had happened during our visit to the high school. I explained the whole situation, making sure he understood why I made the decision to remove her from her school. After I had completed my summary of that early afternoon, he wanted to know what I was going to do next. Feeling somewhat alone in the situation I looked him straight in the eye and said, "I don't know! Help me out here! I just had to get our child out of that school. What is your thinking?"

We spent the next several hours discussing what we should do as a family. Celeste was so glad to be out of there she didn't seem to be concerned that she no longer had a high school to attend. I knew a fifteen year old needed socialization, so we never considered a "home school" option. I also knew that finding a new school would fall to me, since Ben was not a "proactive" type of man. He was laid back about everything, trusting his wife to "handle" it all. It exhausted me just thinking about it.

Six months earlier I had purchased tickets to see Neil Diamond in concert. The concert was that night! I had planned to take Celeste since Ben wasn't interested in seeing Neil Diamond. At this point, the last thing I wanted to do was to drive thirty miles to the concert, at night, in rush hour traffic. I was unsteady both emotionally and physically, wondering if I could make the drive at all. Celeste was only fifteen years old with nothing more than a driver's permit and no experience driving the freeways. Turning the car over to her was not an option.

We talked about cancelling and Celeste said, "Mom, you have been looking forward to this for months. Let's go. You'll be ok."

She had more confidence in me than I had in myself! The last thing you ever want your child to know is that you are scared. With this in mind I just said, "Ok, let's do it."

I was to the point of prayer as I got ready for the evening. I remember the silent plea I sent heavenward, "Please, Lord, help me drive safely to the concert and home again. Give me the strength to handle what needs to be done. And please, show me a way out of this mess."

I marveled at my daughter's cheery demeanor as she got ready for the concert. She not only looked great, but happy and secure that mom seemed to have everything under control. That was so very far from the truth;

## Chapter 9: Angelic Surprise

"Mom" was as frightened as she had ever been. What if I couldn't find a new school for Celeste? What if we had to MOVE? What about her swimming career? All of these questions swirled in my head. I had a heavy heart, and I felt completely alone with this new challenge resting squarely on my shoulders.

We made it safely to the downtown arena. I knew parking would be a problem; but, as luck would have it, a parking place came open very close to the front of the arena! Hurray! We would not be two women walking back to our car alone, 11 PM at night, in a high crime downtown area. This small bit of good fortune turned out to be a precursor to some very interesting events that were about to take place that memorable Friday night.

As we entered the arena, I handed our tickets to the doorman. He quickly gave us instructions to help us navigate our way to our seats. It was a huge place, but we found our assigned seats without a problem. In the hallways outside the seating area, vendors were situated everywhere, creating an overwhelming smell of food that drifted throughout the arena. Since Celeste was feeling so good, she was hungry and wanted to know if she could get us some hamburgers. The Burger King vendor was right outside our portal door, so I said, "Sure. Go get yourself something to eat. I will be right here."

Appearing concerned she asked, "Mom! Have you even eaten today?"

Still feeling a queasy stomach I was quick to reply, "No, the thought of food just doesn't sound good to me right now."

Celeste wouldn't stop. "Mom. You have to eat. Please let me get you a burger too."

I didn't want one, but I said ok, and handed her some cash. As it turned out, our seats were on the very end of the row, so I gazed over at our neighbors to our left. Three women were chatting away seemingly having a wonderful time. I was envious of their joy and thought to myself, "Well, there are probably a lot of happy, excited people here tonight. I will just have to put on my happy face and 'fake it until I make it'."

I wondered when I would ever feel "happy" again. One of the women must have noticed the sorrowful look on my face. She stopped chatting with her friends, leaned over Celeste's empty chair and asked, "Is everything ok with you?"

Suddenly, all three women "tuned in" to her question. I forced a smile, saying, "Actually, no. I just pulled my daughter out of Painted Mountain High School. She is a top-level swimmer and she has been bullied to the point that her life is in danger. The 'word' around the school is that one of the swimmers is dating a gang member and a 'hit' has been put out on my daughter's life because she left the team."

All three women stared at me for what seemed an eternity. I added, "I have no idea where to place her in school next. I understand that the Gilmore School District, the district closest to our home, has a waiting list to get in. I don't know what I am going to do."

What happened next completely startled me. The woman sitting closest to me said, "You are right, Gilmore

Chapter 9: Angelic Surprise

has a waiting list. All three of us teach in the Gilmore district."

I couldn't believe it! What were the chances of being seated next to three Gilmore teachers in an arena filled with 17,000 screaming fans? Celeste, Ben and I had discussed the possibility of getting her into Gilmore High School. It was relatively close and offered a manageable drive to and from school. We knew the school had a good reputation, but we also knew there was a waiting list.

At that point, Celeste arrived with the food. She dove into her hamburger and fries as she handed me my dinner. I chuckled to myself thinking, "I am so glad she seems to be happy and hungry. Personally, I am neither!"

As the band on the circular stage started to play, the arena erupted with screaming and shouting! Neil was about to make his appearance. I quickly whispered to Celeste, "The three ladies next to you teach in the Gilmore School District. Maybe they can help us somehow."

The crowd roared even louder as Neil came on stage. I studied the mixture of people in the audience... everyone seemed to be somewhere in their forties. A few were younger and a few older. Many of us knew the music of Neil Diamond as teenagers. Without doubt we were on a nostalgic trip, turning back the pages to our younger years. What a thrill, here we were, listening to a live performance!

My petite swimmer had literally "inhaled" her entire dinner. I nibbled at my hamburger trying to ignore the fact that my stomach was in a complete knot. The food tasted like glue as I gingerly chewed and tried to swallow.

Even though I just wanted to go back to the car and drive home, I felt myself getting caught up in "Neil Diamond" fever. Slowly, the excitement of the crowd got us up on our feet, clapping and dancing. As I set my hamburger aside I thought, "You know what? My problems will still be here when this concert is over. So, for the rest of the show, I am just going to 'rock it' like everyone else."

Even though Celeste was one of the youngest people in the arena, she was a good sport about letting some "old ladies" have fun. I could tell that the Gilmore group of teachers were "over the top" in their excitement, obviously having a wonderful time. Watching them out of the corner of my eye, I couldn't get over the feeling that they were different somehow. They were animated and excited like they didn't have a care in the world. Their clothing seemed to be a little odd; not particularly stylish and rather outdated.

During intermission none of three got up to leave. They just sat there, happily talking about the first half of the show. Seeing an opportunity to get some more information about Gilmore, I leaned over Celeste and asked the three of them, "Do any of you have any suggestions as to how I might get Celeste enrolled at Gilmore High School?"

Without hesitation, the lady in the middle of the threesome said, "Yes. This is what you must do. You need to 'move' to Gilmore. It's the only way to get your child into the district. You don't need to move there physically. Just get a post office box with a Gilmore address, and act like you live in the city. When you have a Gilmore address, go to the high school and enroll her. They will be glad to have a top swimmer on the team."

Celeste and I stared at one another in disbelief. Hope began to swell in both of our minds. These women had given us a solution and told us how to make it happen! I felt the knot in my stomach relax a bit as Neil made his way back on stage for the second half of the show.

We continued to clap and sing and dance until the show ended. As we were getting ready to leave, I looked over at the three ladies gratefully. I wanted to do something nice for them; a thank you note, some flowers, some little thing to thank them for helping me. I said "Where do you all work? I would like to thank you properly."

All three of them started to laugh and giggle, never answering my question. Once again, I found this behavior to be rather odd. As I gathered up my purse, my uneaten hamburger and my sweater, I turned once again to ask the same question. They were gone! In an instant they had disappeared into a gridlock of 17,000 people waiting to find the exits. I knew it would take at least thirty minutes to get out of the stadium; still, the three teachers were nowhere to be seen. They seemed to have "vanished" into thin air. I looked at Celeste and asked, "Did you see them leave? How did they get out of here so fast?"

She just looked at me with wide eyes and exclaimed, "I have no idea how they got out of here. We can hardly move an inch!"

Being a woman of faith, and always open to miracles large and small, I asked Celeste, "Do you remember the quote from the Bible that warns, 'Be kind to everyone, for you may never know when you are in the company of angels'?"

With a smile I added, "I believe we just met some angels. They will certainly always be angels to me!" A smile lit up Celeste's face as we started the lengthy process of making our way out of the arena and back to the car.

## Chapter Ten
# The Tough Go Shopping

I BARELY SLEPT THAT FRIDAY NIGHT. I spent a lot of time wandering around the house thinking about the plan the three "angels" had suggested. I checked on Celeste several times and found her sleeping peacefully. I looked at Ben, who was sound asleep, asking myself, "How can he sleep at a time like this?"

As I paced back and forth it occurred to me that a post office box in Gilmore was certainly possible. I remembered visiting a shipping outlet store in Gilmore that had a number of P.O. boxes for rent. What really bothered me was a nagging thought that we might have to prove we actually "lived" in the community. Considering the cost of home rentals, we would have to settle for something not much larger than the proverbial "shoe box."

The next day I asked Ben if he knew anyone who had a permanent residence in Gilmore. He said, "Sure.

Charles lives there. He is divorced and lives alone in a huge house."

Charles was Ben's immediate supervisor at work. Having met him just once I asked, "Do you think I could get him to sign a false rental agreement? One that said Celeste and I were renting 'space' from him?"

Ben said he would ask him the following Monday. When Monday finally arrived, and Celeste crawled out of bed, I made her a big breakfast. Cooking had always been a good way for me to relieve some stress when I was tense. I tried to eat some breakfast myself, but it just wasn't happening. I thought, "Gee, at this rate I will get down to that elusive 'size six' in no time at all."

I remembered that Celeste had not told me what happened at the high school meeting on Friday afternoon. I could tell it was hard for her to share what had happened, but I needed to know. Although she wasn't aware of it, I had been keeping notes about all the negative episodes, rumors, lies, stolen items, and people who had harmed us in some way. I was building a case with as much information as possible since I planned to see an attorney when things settled down.

In answer to my question, Celeste began to tell me her story. "Mom, I went in there knowing that the coaches knew you planned to pull me off the team. There was lots of yelling and I was pushed up against the door so I couldn't get out of the office. I was told that it would be our fault if they did not win anything at the State Championships. I don't remember a lot of what was said except at the very end I heard, 'Let me tell you something

Celeste, when you grow older and move away from home your mommy is not going to be there to bail you out of every situation. I hope you understand that!'"

Celeste continued, "All I could think about was getting out of that office. It was horrible. I didn't want you to know what happened in there."

Hearing those ugly words, I felt like a dagger had been plunged into my heart. I was shocked and enraged. I could not believe that such a blatant lack of professionalism had been directed toward a fifteen year old girl. As a teacher myself, this was unthinkable! I had occasionally felt anger toward children in a classroom; but, I would never, under any circumstances, have inflicted my rage upon a student. I sat quietly for awhile. This alarmed Celeste as she asked, "Mom! Why are you so quiet? You're scaring me. What are you going to do?"

I replied, "I am not sure; but, I have a notebook full of things that have been happening to you and me. This offense, one that was aimed directly at you by a professional, is going into my notes in capital letters!"

I looked forward to sharing this story with a close girlfriend of mine. We ate at the same restaurant each week, exchanging stories about our families and friends. My friend Mary and her husband were both aware of the pain we were enduring as we supported Celeste's swimming career. Like all good friends they had been a tremendous support. Since I was having problems getting food down, I wanted to cancel our lunch that day. But, I knew my friend would have something wise to say, so I kept our lunch date.

I repeated the story about what Celeste had endured during that final meeting at the high school when she was pushed up against the door when trying to leave. Upon hearing this, Mary put down her fork with disgust and exclaimed, "Leslie, write all of this down. When things settle down, you pay a visit to the Superintendent of Public Instruction. Whoever did this should be fired for behaving that way toward your child!"

Wow! She was serious and probably correct. At that particular point in time, I simply did not have enough "fight" left in me to make that kind of move. I was truly in "survival" mode, making an effort to place one foot in front of the other. When I got back home, I did "log" my friend's impassioned statement into my notebook for consideration at a later time.

On my way home, I stopped at the Dairy Queen to get Celeste one of her favorite "goodies," a Peanut Buster Parfait. After she had consumed this sizable ice cream treat, I had an idea. "Celeste! Let's go shopping!"

This was one of those "out of the box" moments. Normally, I disliked malls and Celeste would have to plead with me to go shopping with her. Her response was, "Are you kidding? You hate shopping!"

I couldn't suppress a smile as I said, "Let me put it this way. If 'they' are going to hate us, and 'they' do, they are going to have to hate us looking gorgeous!"

Celeste was on her way to the car before I could change my mind. We visited our favorite "discount" store where we felt we could get the most for our money.

We toured the store, tried things on and loaded up our shopping basket. For the first time in my marriage, I bought whatever the two of us wanted. My husband was extremely frugal and I knew I would have some explaining to do. But, I felt good about this little adventure! It was great fun watching Celeste buy what pleased her; I couldn't help but remember a version of the old saw, "When the going gets tough, the tough go shopping."

After arriving home, we put on our own private "fashion show." This was great fun because both of us had the opportunity to try all of our new things on again. When Ben arrived home from his day at the shooting range, I let him relax awhile before I told him about our "little adventure." Instead of feeling guilty, or hiding anything, I simply told him the truth. "Celeste and I went shopping and we spent quite a bit of money. But you know what? We both needed to do something nice for ourselves after enduring this horrible ordeal. And it's not over yet."

Ben didn't say anything…a common reaction for him much of the time. I let the news sink in while I put my new things away. I was thankful that Ben had not raised a fuss. Regardless, I couldn't get rid of a nagging feeling of uncertainty about Celeste's future. It was Saturday, and I could not move forward with any plans until Monday.

On Sunday, Celeste and I went to church at my request. I needed to spend some time in a holy space with the hope of gaining some clarity about our situation. I felt it would be nothing short of miraculous if our family could survive what was ahead without any lasting scars. I was counting on help from a "Higher Power" to help me figure out our next move.

## Chapter Eleven
# Moving to Gilmore

When Monday morning arrived, I called Ben at work to see if he had spoken with his supervisor. He said he had not seen him yet but would be sure to talk with him before the end of the day.

Celeste slept later than normal that Monday, knowing she didn't have to go to school or swim practice. I was not accustomed to having her home all day during the school year. The fact that she loved to read was a blessing because I had always limited the use of television during the day. Those were the days before the electronic explosion, so cell phones and computers were not constant companions for most teenagers.

I did make a call to her beloved USS Club coach that day. I knew he would be deeply saddened to hear that Celeste would not be swimming with him or the club anymore. He was a good man, with Celeste's best interests at heart. Although he appreciated and enhanced her skills in the pool, he never exploited her talent. I explained briefly what was happening while admitting that I did not know what we were going to do next. I promised to keep him informed. I heard deep sorrow and concern in his voice when he wished us well. He was fond of Celeste and I knew he was truly troubled by what was happening to her.

My sister was due to arrive the next day from a small, northern California mountain community. She was pregnant with my niece and was looking forward to some time in our "sun belt" state away from the brutally cold mountain weather. I was in "overload" mode emotionally, and I knew that Katie would not understand the bullying behavior that my child was enduring. My first thought was to ask her to come at a better time; but, we were close sisters and I did not want to hurt her. It wasn't long before I began to think of her as a "help" mate. Perhaps she could help with shopping and cooking while I concentrated on our immediate problems. I decided not to say anything; I would just pick her up at the airport as planned.

Celeste spent the day relaxing and taking it easy. It was a joy to see her so happy, but the reality was that each day she spent out of school would roll over into absenteeism wherever she attended school next. I kept that worry to myself, simply letting her enjoy her days of freedom.

Ben called mid-afternoon with the message, "Could you and Celeste meet with Charles and me after work? He would like to have a beer and the chance to meet the two of you before he considers 'renting' you space at his home."

Charles had never met Celeste, so it was quite reasonable to give him an opportunity to know what kind of person she was, as well as hear more about why we needed to make this kind of "move."

We met at 4:30 that afternoon at Charles's favorite restaurant close to where he and Ben worked. Charles ordered a beer for the adults and a Coke for Celeste. Charles had an adult daughter of his own, so he knew how to talk to a fifteen year old girl. Celeste turned on the charm and chatted amiably with Charles. Ben and I just listened as the two of them got to know one another. I commented appropriately, but I let Celeste tell him the story about what had happened to her. At the end of our visit, Charles shook Celeste's hand, then mine, and said, "I would be more than happy to have you two as 'faux' renters. Just bring me a contract, take a 'tour' of the house, and we will fill in the numbers at that time."

I felt happier than I had in months. Things finally seemed to be falling into place. We said goodbye and headed home. Ben told me later that Charles was exceptionally impressed with our daughter. That was a much needed "motherhood moment" for me!

Now that it appeared that we might have a place to "live" in Gilmore, my plan was to stop by the shipping store in Gilmore the next morning before picking up my sister at the airport. I would rent a post office box and pick up a rental agreement to take to Charles. I had seen those kinds of contracts at stationery stores, so I would check there first thing in the morning. Part of my plan was to take things slowly, taking care not to rush the process. We would just "disappear" from the whole swimming and school "scene," letting those who wanted to hurt Celeste wonder what had happened to us. We would just slowly "resurface" when it was safe to do so.

On Tuesday morning, Celeste and I rented a post office box at the shipping store in Gilmore. We needed a permanent "home" address, so I put down Charles's street address even though we had not formally rented space from him. It never occurred to me that I would feel guilty about lying; but, I justified my actions by thinking that this whole charade would provide greater safety for my daughter.

We were given our post office box number and its keys. The owner of the store was young and very friendly with Celeste. It gave me deep pleasure to watch her personality re-emerge as she talked to people with whom she felt safe. They chatted about starting high school in the Gilmore school district. He asked if we had just moved to Gilmore. We both said "YES!" in tandem, changing the subject immediately. Hmmmm. I hoped the "fibbing" would become easier the more I practiced.

The next stop was the stationery store where I had seen do-it-yourself contract agreements for sale. I found divorce packets, wills, power of attorney, and finally a generic rental agreement that would serve our purpose. We bought one and added it to our growing stack of "Gilmore" paperwork. We then headed to the airport to pick up my sister Katie.

## Chapter 11: Moving to Gilmore

When we arrived at the airport, I remembered that I had not mentioned to my sister that Celeste would be with me. Thinking ahead, I decided I would tell her Celeste's entire story over a large cup of coffee while Celeste was busy doing other things. Katie had been an athlete in high school and was still an avid runner and skier. I wasn't sure whether she had any idea about harassment in the world of sports, but she was about to find out.

As Katie walked through the secured gate area, a big smile lit up her face when she saw Celeste and me waiting for her. She looked happy, but confused as to why Celeste was with me. I gave her a hug and told her I would explain why Celeste wasn't in school a little later. I marveled at her little baby "bump" and felt so happy for her. She had tried to have a child for twelve years; finally, it was going to happen! I looked forward to my new role as "Auntie Les."

Both Katie and Celeste were hungry, so we stopped at a nearby Mexican restaurant. The two of them ate a huge lunch while I nibbled on a taco. I knew I was still "on edge" because I had never had a problem getting food down. Normally, I loved to eat, and the fact that everything tasted the same was not a good sign. I was still trying to protect Celeste from my concerns and so far it was working. However, the decreasing numbers on my bathroom scale told a different story. A stress diet is never a good way to lose weight; but, I was doing the best I could do in the food department.

That day, the weather was nice enough for us to sit outside in the evening so Katie and I took our drinks out by the pool. I began to tell her the whole story. When I was done she was somewhat shocked, but she knew more about bullying than I had expected. Her husband, Celeste's uncle, had been an Olympic swimming hopeful and had experienced some of the behavior I just described. Fortunately, her husband had been able to "manage" his tormenters until they stopped their bad behavior. It seemed to me that he was one of the lucky ones.

Later that evening I called Charles, our new "landlord," to see if we could arrange a time to see his house and sign the contract. He said Wednesday evening would be fine, so we set a time. I wondered what kind of home he had, and what neighborhood "we" would be claiming as our own. When he gave me a gate code I knew he must live in a very nice area.

It was that time of year when the state fair was in full swing. Celeste and I had always gone to the fair. We enjoyed the carnival atmosphere and the opportunity to see all of the animals. I felt sure my sister would enjoy it too, so I asked if she would like to tag along. She thought it sounded like great fun.

We had never attended the fair on a weekday because Celeste was always in school. Since that was not a factor this week, we set off to the state fair on a bright Wednesday morning. As we wandered around looking at the animals and displays, we filled our mouths with typical fair food. One of my favorites was the oh-so-good, gigantic cinnamon roll. As the three of us were busy consuming these luscious treats, a security guard approached us and asked, "Do you girls know how many calories are in those things?"

I just smiled and answered, "Yes we do, and right now, we don't care!"

I found myself spoiling Celeste throughout the day by letting her have almost anything she wanted. She said to me months later, "Mother, I just loved that week when I slept in every day, and you bought me whatever I wanted…it was great!!" It didn't feel "great" to me at the time, but I was glad she remembered it that way.

That evening we were due at Charles's house at 6 PM. I left my pregnant sister in charge of the family dinner while Celeste and I went to see our new "digs." I had a map that helped me make my way through an unfamiliar part of Gilmore where his house was located. When we found his gated area, we stopped at the keypad to put in the entry code he had given us. As the huge, heavy gates slowly swung open we drove through some large arches into the housing area itself. I exclaimed, "Wow! Looks like we will be living (on paper) in the high-rent district!" Celeste showed the same surprise as we made our way by beautiful homes situated on the edge of a long, winding lake. What fun it was to see people's boats tied up to docks in front of their houses.

Charles met us at the front door and I couldn't help gushing about the beauty of the neighborhood! He chuckled and was humble about his home. When we stepped inside we saw that the interior was as beautiful as the exterior. Even though he didn't have a boat, the view of the lake was stunning. Bringing myself back to reality,

I pulled out the generic rental agreement and we began to study its contents. One of the first things we would have to do was to decide on a rental amount. After a little discussion he came up with a figure that sounded reasonable to me. After answering a few more questions we signed the contract.

I was thankful to have this milestone out of the way, but part of me was unnerved. I had just signed a legal document saying I would be paying rent every month! Charles could have demanded payment, but I had a feeling he truly wanted to help Celeste and would never consider doing that to us. I thanked him profusely and drove back past the lake, under the arch and out the gate.

Katie had dinner under control when we returned, so we sat down to eat as a family. It felt good having my sister's emotional support as I mentally worked through some of the changes that were ahead. I would be enrolling Celeste at her new high school on Friday, so we "girls" talked about what we might do for fun on Thursday. I knew my sister was not familiar with any of the pretty lakes in our state, so we made plans to check out a boat ride the next day.

When we arrived at the lake closest to home the next morning, we saw an old Mississippi-style stern wheeler about to depart on a tour. We ran over to the little pay booth on the shore and bought our tickets. How lovely it was to have the three of us—my sister, my daughter and I—about to begin a little adventure on this beautiful desert lake. For a couple of hours we relaxed and enjoyed a slow moving panorama of stately saguaro cactuses framed by rugged cliffs and a cloud-dotted sky.

I was still battling my nervous tummy, but I couldn't let it slow me down. I had one more "hurdle" to overcome that week. That would be the day we enrolled Celeste in her new school. Until that time came, I just concentrated on enjoying a beautiful day on the lake, surrounded by two people I dearly loved.

## Chapter Twelve
# A Fresh Start

On Friday morning, Katie was enjoying coffee in our backyard, taking in the sunshine. Celeste and I dressed and we got ready to go to Gilmore High School to enroll her as a new student. I told my sister that I wasn't sure when we would be back, but we would think of something fun to do together that afternoon. We gathered all of the important documents we would need to enroll Celeste and put them in a folder to take with us. As I headed toward the high school, our first appointment was to meet her new principal at 10 AM. I felt Celeste would feel more comfortable if she met the main administrator at her new school.

We knew where the high school was located; I had driven Celeste by the school several times to make sure she was familiar with the new location. I also needed to "adjust" to this change because I would be making this ten mile drive twice a day to deliver my daughter and pick her up again. I had been a "driving" mom for so long a little more driving didn't seem to matter. My desire to keep my daughter safe from harm seemed far more important than building mileage on my car or the requirement for two more hours of my time.

The route we took to the high school was a very scenic drive. Gilmore was still mainly a farming area, with a variety of crops growing beside the road as well as several working dairy farms. We also saw many large homes majestically situated on very large pieces of property. Even though Gilmore had some master planned communities like the one we were "renting" from Charles, it was still a very "rural" area. The many horse properties gave a feeling of spaciousness, unlike the congested "built-up" area where we lived a few miles north.

We arrived at the principal's office a little before 10 in the morning. His secretary was kind, and told us that he would be out to greet us shortly. I had a running dialog going on in my head as I mentally rehearsed answering any questions he might ask. "What brought you to the Gilmore area?" "Where do you work?" I was making myself sick knowing I would have to falsify some of my answers. I did some deep breathing to calm myself before the "Inquisition."

After a few minutes, the principal came out to greet us, motioning us to follow him into his office. Thinking back, I honestly felt like I had been a naughty girl and had been sent to the principal's office for punishment! That had never happened to me as a child, so this was

## Chapter 12: A Fresh Start

truly my first "trip to see the principal!" I couldn't shake the feeling of being in "trouble" somehow.

Fortunately, he directed most of his questions and comments to Celeste. As a result, I was able to sit there quietly, listening to the conversation. Celeste carried the conversation like a pro. I was amazed, and grateful, that I did not need to say much. I still felt unsteady and concerned about accidentally "revealing" our huge secret. Sadly, that feeling remained very much a part of my life for the next three years. I was terrified we would be "found out" and Celeste would be forced back into her former high school of bullying terror.

After completing our visit with the principal, we were sent to the nurse's office to show her that Celeste had her current vaccinations. I knew that proof-of-vaccination would be part of the enrollment process because we had just been through that at her former high school. I had kept good records and all of her shots were recorded in a little book that I had saved from her infancy. As we sat in the nurse's office, that same dark feeling of deceit, or tripping up over our "lie," came over me. Celeste was proving herself to be a very fine actress as she rattled off our new street address and post office box number. The nurse was kind and asked if Celeste felt ok about this change in school halfway through the first semester. She smiled, and said quite convincingly, "Yes! I can't wait to start school here!"

Ms. Nurse turned her gaze toward me. She said, "Mom, you don't look like you are feeling too well. Would you like something to eat or drink?"

I had been caught! My angst was detected by one very astute school nurse! I stammered, "Ahhh, sure… whatever you have would be nice."

She left the room and quickly returned with orange juice, graham crackers and some peanut butter. I really did feel like a small child again as I ate this little protein snack. I think I had completely forgotten to eat breakfast, so it actually tasted very good. A little "pampering" from a kind professional was exactly what I needed.

When we left her office, Celeste put her arm through mine. For once, the tables had turned and she was strong when I felt weak. She said, "Mom! It's going to be ok. We can do this!"

As I looker over at her and smiled I thought to myself, "We have to do this. We have no other choice."

The next stop was the enrollment office where Celeste was to meet with her counselor. The woman at the front desk motioned to two empty chairs in front of her desk. When we sat down, she handed me a stack of paperwork to fill out. As I began to look over the contents of the package, she added, "Before you fill out the forms I will need proof of residency in our school district to put in Celeste's file."

I froze as I stared at the paperwork in front of me. Celeste saw the look on my face and quickly reached into our folder to find the rental agreement we had created with Charles. The woman thanked her and went into a back office to make a photocopy. While she was gone, Celeste helped me fill out the paperwork, whispering our address and p.o. box to me, since my mind didn't seem to be working properly. I wondered to myself if I was developing some sort of dementia, but decided to label my confusion as nothing more than a stress reaction.

When the woman returned, she handed back the rental agreement and I gave her the paperwork to add to Celeste's folder. We were then asked to sit in some other chairs until her counselor was ready to see her. I tried to keep a "poker" face, looking as calm as possible. We were so close to being finished with the enrollment process I didn't want anything to interfere.

Celeste's counselor appeared and greeted us warmly. She was kind and seemed very sympathetic toward a sophomore who was starting in a new school at age fifteen. Because there was overcrowding in the district, and the semester had already begun, class choices were limited. Celeste told her what classes she had been taking at her former high school as they considered available choices. The only major change in schedule was a history class that students normally take in their junior year. Celeste felt comfortable with this change, so she was placed in the class. The counselor wondered aloud about the necessary physical education credits. I quickly said, "I want her to take a break from physical education until next year. She is currently swimming on a United States Swim Team."

With this comment the counselor suddenly came alive as she exclaimed, "We have a good swim team here at Gilmore high school, and we could certainly use some more swimmers! Let me call the athletic director and see if he is in."

Once again I sat stiffly as I ran our options through my mind. I hoped and prayed he would be too busy to see us. When I glanced at Celeste I could see that she looked a little panicked as well. The counselor hung up the phone and said, "When we are done here, he said to come on down to see him! It's not too late to put her on the swim team here in Gilmore!"

Good grief. I had just pulled her off her last high school team and I was certainly not going to put her on an opposing high school team two weeks before the finals! I kept thinking, "Play the game Leslie…play the game and make it swing in Celeste's favor."

Fortunately, Celeste had not told her counselor about the bullying problem she was facing. She must have sensed that it was a good time to remain quiet and let "Mom" figure out the next step. The counselor made sure her schedule would work time-wise. Another major consideration was a schedule that would avoid putting Celeste too far behind in her school work. As we double checked the classes, I was still having trouble "focusing" and just prayed that her class schedule would be adequate.

When the two of them were satisfied with the schedule, she told Celeste where she could find her locker. She assured Celeste that she could visit her anytime, with any kind of problem. That last comment was a comfort to both of us because she seemed to really mean it. I was numb when we stood to say goodbye, realizing we now we had to face a new athletic director. I was thinking to myself, "Why does everyone seem so interested in my child's swimming talent? What if she had learned to play the tuba? No one would try to make her play the tuba just because she was good at it!!!"

## Chapter 12: A Fresh Start

I chuckled to myself thinking, "I guess I really haven't lost my mind. I can still laugh!"

We headed out the door and down the stairs to find the athletic director's office. I could feel the blood leave my face when Celeste asked, "Mom! Is he going to make me swim? That means I would have to face the team of bullies that I just left!"

I hated this look of fear on her face: I had seen it too many times. I said firmly, "Absolutely not. We will give him a 'bare bones' report of what has happened to you, and I will just say 'No, not this season. Thank you, and goodbye.' Don't worry Celeste, we almost have you enrolled. We are very close to a new beginning."

The athletic director's office was large with several windows facing the hallway. I could see him talking on the phone as we approached the door. He was a big, burley man who looked like someone you might find in a boxing ring rather than a high school office. He waved us in as he continued to talk on the phone. I remember silently praying for the courage to stand firm against this man if he wanted my daughter to swim. He hung up the phone and we all shook hands with one another. His first sentence was aimed directly at Celeste, not her mom. After all, she was fifteen and was fully capable of holding her own. The director's first words were, "So, I hear you are a very good swimmer! We would be very happy to have you swim for us! I can call the swim coach right now and you can start practice next week!"

I waited for what seemed an eternity expecting Celeste to say something. This time she froze! Since she apparently didn't know what to say, I decided to give an overview of our bullying story as gently as I could. "You need to know a little bit about why we are here, and why Celeste has changed schools halfway through the first semester. Because Celeste excelled at swimming, at both at her high school and her USS teams, she became the object of severe bullying by her teammates. It became so bad that it was rumored that if she left the team, a 'contract' would be put on her life by a teammate dating a gang member. We moved to Gilmore to get her away from this extreme bullying and the possibility that her life is in danger. Please know that I am not exaggerating! The bullying didn't happen overnight, but it slowly spiraled out of control as she continued to excel in her sport. I do not want her to swim at all until everything settles down, if and when that occurs. In addition to enrolling her here, I also plan to find her a new USS team when we have 'recovered' from this current mess."

I watched a look of shock slowly cover his face as if to say, "Who would do this to such a nice kid?" His next words were very kind. Speaking directly to Celeste he said, "I am so sorry to hear this. This should never have happened to you and I can understand your reluctance to join our team at this point. I wish you well and come and see me next fall if and when you are ready to swim again. Thank you for coming in to see me. Good luck to both of you!"

Celeste and I breathed a sigh of relief. This large, loud man obviously had a heart of gold. I was grateful that he had shown compassion toward my child. I had done "battle" with too many professionals in the past and I appreciated someone who actually listened to me and acknowledged my concerns. We all stood to shake hands as we left. He even gave Celeste a little pat on the back as we left his office.

The bell rang just as we entered the main hall on our way to the front of the school. Doors flew open and students seemed to be everywhere all at once! I felt like a fish swimming upstream against a "current" of students going the opposite direction. I was the target of quite a few disparaging looks that asked the question, "What is a MOTHER doing in here??"

Through the din of chattering high school students, I shouted to Celeste, "Before we leave, why don't we make sure you can find your way around this huge place next Monday. It would also be a good idea to try your locker to make sure it works."

She thought that was a good idea. When we finally made our way to the front door of the school, we turned around and began our search for her many class rooms. We made this circuit several times until she felt comfortable with each of their locations. I found her "peering" into a few classrooms to get a "feel" for the new groups of students she would be meeting on the following Monday. I was looking forward to her meeting new girlfriends who would replace those who had betrayed her. I was proud to see her showing a "no fear" attitude toward this change. She was clearly ready to start over again and I had every hope that it would be a good fit for her.

When we located her locker, we were pleased to find that it was empty and the combination lock worked just fine. (Sometimes students were forced to share lockers due to the overcrowding problem.) It had been quite an eventful morning and we were both ready to go home. I knew my sister would be ready to see us, and anxious to hear all about our latest "adventure." Getting in the car, we made our way back through the colorful farmlands that surrounded the school. Turning north, we headed for home.

Katie was anxiously waiting to hear all about what had taken place. When Celeste was busy in her room, I began a blow-by-blow description of our experiences. When I finished I said, "The school is just huge with thousands of students. Personally, I would be terrified to tackle that crowd, but Celeste seems at peace with the challenge. I think she is so thrilled to be out of danger that she is willing to manage anything."

Katie looked pleased, obviously happy for her niece. Since we had been able to accomplish all of these activities in the morning, I asked my sister what she would like to do that afternoon. She quickly asked, "Would you mind taking me to the mall? I need some new maternity things and I don't have this kind of shopping at home."

I knew Celeste would love another trip to the mall. I had never been much of a shopper, but I knew it would be fun for both of my "girls" that afternoon.

We decided to shop at one of our newest malls. It was one of the finest in the city and my sister had never been there. I was sure we could find what she wanted.

To make our shopping trip a little more exciting, we had lunch in the food court knowing that Celeste was enjoying one of her last afternoons of freedom playing "hooky" from school.

After visiting all of the anchor stores and one maternity shop, we all began to feel the effects of tired feet. I had forgotten that they had a beautiful old carousel in that mall, but I spotted it as we were headed back to the mall exit. The "child" in me couldn't stand it. I said, "Would you two mind if I took a ride on the carousel?"

I thought that might embarrass both of them, but in unison they chorused, "No! Let's all ride!"

So the three of us–one pregnant sister, one happy daughter, and one exhausted mom–climbed aboard. We were the only adults riding without a small child, but none of us seemed to care. As the carousel began to move, a "view of the future" entered my mind. I saw that my sister was "riding" toward a new life with a beloved baby girl-to-be, while Celeste was riding toward a new circle of friends and new connections. As the music of the carousel carried me atop my "white stallion," I mused that my work was not yet over regarding my daughter. She still had three years of high school left and I knew my "vigil" would not be over for awhile. I was happy in that moment, but still uncertain of Celeste's future. I made an effort to simply remain in the moment, enjoy the ride, and not think any further ahead than, "What shall we have for dinner this evening?"

**Chapter Thirteen**

# A New Team

Celeste began class work at her new high school the following Monday. We put my sister on the plane Sunday afternoon, with plans to spend the rest of the day picking out new school supplies. Excited at the opportunity, Celeste found all of her materials and carefully picked just the right outfit to wear the next day.

When Monday arrived, we completed the ten-mile drive to her new school in plenty of time for her to find her first class before the bell rang. As she climbed out of the car in front of the school, I found myself saying a prayer for her, "Please, Lord, make this transition as painless as possible. Give her courage to be friendly and meet new people. Thank You!"

Celeste gave me a little "peck" on the cheek as she got out of the car. I was pleased with this show of affection considering the tough day that lay ahead. As I watched her walk away, she melted into the crowd of students. I found myself having some "separation anxiety," much like the time she started kindergarten! We had spent so much time together the last few weeks that it was hard letting her go again. When I returned home, the dog and I took a very long walk. Physical exercise had always cleared my mind and helped me relax.

When I arrived to pick up Celeste that afternoon, I searched a sea of students to find my daughter in the crowd. When I did see her, she was smiling broadly. Apparently the day had gone well with no major problems. She seemed to like all of her teachers, which pleased me, and she told me that the students were very friendly and welcoming. This even included some of the older swimmers she knew from her USS swim meets. Even though most of them were on opposing teams, it was nice that they were friendly and supportive. Because she seemed happy and content, I felt myself relax a bit. Hopefully we had made a good decision.

Now that Celeste was not swimming on a high school team, the high school swimming championships were going to proceed without my daughter's participation. Early one Saturday morning, as I was comfortably reading the morning paper in bed, Celeste came in and sat at the foot of my bed. After a few seconds hesitation she said, "I want to go watch the finals."

I just stared at her. "You mean you want to go sit in the stands and watch everyone else swim without you?"

## Chapter 13: A New Team

My voice was louder than normal. Without hesitation she answered, "Yes. I want to watch them swim without me."

I was incredulous! I couldn't believe it! That was the last thing I wanted to do. I did not want to be near any of those parents, bullies or coaches! I was quiet as I thought things through. Then, I said, "Well, if that is what you want to do, count me in!"

Part of me was proud of her. What courage! Even though I was worried that someone might harm her, I figured that they would have to get to me first. There might be some risk involved, but I wanted to support my daughter's decision. I felt like a member of the CIA, ready to "take the hit" for my brave daughter. I quickly banished that thought from my mind. I would not let fear rule my emotions. We would be fine, and, we would be strong.

When we arrived at the large swimming complex thirty minutes from our home, some of her former teammates were passing out programs at the gate. We smiled, took a program, and left them standing there with their mouths open. As we made our way into the grandstand, parents and swimmers alike had stunned looks on their faces. We found a rather secluded place to sit by ourselves. I knew we weren't welcome, and I wanted plenty of distance between us and any unsavory characters that might show up. I could see the gossip mongers staring at us, whispering and passing the news along. "Celeste and her mom are here! Can you believe it?"

I was thinking to myself, "We are not going away. Even though Celeste is not swimming, we have every right to watch these finals. So be it."

We watched as Celeste's former high school team was badly beaten. There was no joy in that fact, only sadness. I thought to myself, "You people wanted her gone. Now you have no way to win any of the relays without her. Looks like you shot yourselves in the foot."

I watched Celeste's face during the meet. To my surprise she was without emotion as she watched her former team's poor performance. We were not there to gloat, or to take pleasure in the losses, our silent but profound message was simply; "We are not going away. We are making major changes to ensure Celeste's safety, but she will still be swimming on a new United States Swim team, and perhaps her new high school swim team next year. Get used to it!"

At the end of the meet we remained silent, speaking to no one. It wasn't necessary to say a thing. They saw us, and we were there, brave and strong. No one was going to take our power away again. In that moment, I was proud that my daughter and I had become a formidable team. We made our way out of the stadium and back to the car. After the car doors were shut and locked, we did a little "high five." We were both amazed that we had actually been there. We were equally amazed that we had remained composed and unfazed. Hurray for us!

For about one month, Celeste was without either a USS team or a high school swim team. She was making new friends at school and seemed content. She also managed to catch up with her school work as reflected in her last progress report.

At home, Celeste was spending more time than I liked in front of the television set, so one afternoon I asked if she was ready to begin swimming with a new United States Swim team. I didn't want her to feel pressured, so I assured her it was strictly up to her if she wanted to start again. She readily admitted that she missed swim practice and was ready to find a new team.

I had been watching all of the other USS teams at the major meets, knowing that someday we might need to make a change. Some families were "team hoppers"; they moved their children on and off of teams according to which coach had the most swimmers with National qualifying times. Since "times" were not important to our family, we would use other criteria for our selection.

Based on my past experience, I knew that any "out of city" team we chose would require substantial driving time to and from practice. I was ready to be the "swim mom" again because I did not want my child to have too much free time. I wanted Celeste to be too busy to get into trouble. I had always felt that way, and was willing to sacrifice more of my time toward this goal.

There was a small team southwest of our city that had caught my attention. They were a fairly new team and the coach-to-swimmer ratio was good. I had noticed that the swimmers seemed like a little "family," often sitting together under one of their two pretty shade canopies. I knew the team name and the coach's name from printed materials that were posted at meets.

One Monday, after delivering Celeste to her high school, I returned home and made the call to the team's coach. I was all prepared to explain who we were and why we needed to make a change. When the coach answered the phone I said, "Hello. My name is Leslie Wood…"

Before I could say another word he exclaimed, "Celeste Wood's mother?"

I was surprised as I asked, "How do you know her?"

He replied, "Mrs. Wood, all of the coaches know her. She was the freshman who came out of nowhere, nearly winning the 5A 50 freestyle last year. We were all there to see it and we knew nothing about her. We do now!"

Encouraged by his enthusiastic response I said, "Well, I have moved her to a new high school, and I need to change her affiliation with United States Swimming as well. Do you have time to see me for breakfast sometime this week?"

With an obvious smile in his voice he asked, "How about tomorrow morning?"

After a few more words, we agreed to meet at a restaurant half way between the thirty miles that separated us.

When I picked Celeste up that afternoon, I told her about meeting the coach on Tuesday. She showed real excitement as she said, "Oh Mom! I think that would be a good fit for me. It's a small team…maybe I will have some friends again."

I knew how important "friends" were during the teenage years, but it still touched me that friends were high on Celeste's priority list. My priorities for the new coach were a bit different: are you going to coach my

## Chapter 13: A New Team

child fairly, without pushing her too hard, and without using bullying techniques to make her National times?" I kept those concerns to myself.

When I arrived for our meeting the next day, the head coach was already there. We shook hands as I sat down across the table. He had brought what looked like reams of paperwork with him. After ordering some food, he began to show me all of the statistics he kept on each swimmer. He wanted me to see that all of his swimmers had improved their times over the course of the two years he had been coaching them. I listened, and then briefly explained what had happened to Celeste. He promised me that he would keep a close eye on any bullying behavior and, if necessary, stop it immediately. He was a very large man, and I felt that he probably had good "control" over his team. He seemed sincere as he asked if I would like to bring Celeste over to the practice pool to meet him and the team before making a decision. I liked that idea, so we made plans to meet at practice that evening. An evening practice would mean night driving for me, but I was willing to do that if she liked the group.

When Celeste returned from school, I told her about our meeting and his invitation to meet him and the team during the late afternoon. This excited Celeste, so she worked hard finishing homework so we could get out of the house by 5 PM. I left some food for Ben's dinner and off we went during rush hour traffic to the new pool.

The new club trained at a local university campus where Celeste and I marveled at the luxurious locker rooms that college swimmers enjoyed. We made our way onto the kool deck where the new coach and team were doing stretching exercises. The head coach smiled when he saw us. I stayed on one side of the pool as Celeste walked over to meet him and the other swimmers. The new coach introduced her to the team, and then sent the team into the pool to warm up while he continued to talk with Celeste. I watched the body language between the two of them carefully. I wanted her to really like her coach so she could begin enjoying her sport again. After about thirty minutes, they stopped talking and she walked back toward me. The coach returned to his teams' activities as we walked out to the car. "Did you like him? Did the other swimmers seem nice? Do you want to join the team?"

I was chattering a mile a minute while she stayed very quiet. I was ready to hear her say "No." Finally, she smiled at me and happily announced, "I'm starting with my new team tomorrow. I need to go home and pack up my swim bag!"

In little more than one month, we had pulled her out of her high school, found a new one, pulled her off her USS team, and found a new USS swim team thirty minutes away. There was still the "fear" that someone might try to hurt her: the world of swimming was a small community and I wouldn't be able to watch over her like before. Once again, a prayer came to mind as we drove home for the evening. "Lord, we are making another major change here. First and foremost, please keep my daughter safe from harm. Let her new coach be a professional and act as such; and, let her have some fun in the pool again."

We had worked hard to get to this place. I had nothing but good hope that this latest change would be a positive one for all of us. I'm not certain, but I like to think that God was smiling down upon us that night as if to say, "You've done good work!"

## Chapter Fourteen
# Junior Nationals

Once again I had become the quintessential "Driving Mom." During school days I spent two hours, morning and afternoon, driving Celeste to and from her high school. Then, at 5 PM, we would leave home and drive thirty minutes during rush hour to practice at the university. She practiced from six to eight in the evening, and sometimes longer, so we would arrive back home around nine o'clock. Ben was usually asleep when we arrived home, so the two of us would put together some kind of "quick" dinner before heading to bed. I became a very good "short order" cook.

During the time Celeste was at swim practice, I had two hours to read or do needlework. Most of the families lived close to the practice pool so they just dropped their swimmers off and picked them up two hours later. It was much too long a drive for me to go home and come back, so I just stayed at the pool while she swam. While I was there, I smiled and did my best to be friendly with everyone. I was trying to give Celeste a lot of "space" to allow her to make friends on her own. Most of the time, I sat in the bleachers, listening to the sound of the water and the coach's instructions to his swimmers. He was quite "business-like" in his coaching style; but, when his swimmers performed well during practice, he would take them into the diving well to play water polo for fun. It was great to see kids just being kids and having a good time. The familiar sound of swimmers doing laps in the pool always brought me pleasure. For some reason, the sound of splashing water seems soothing, whether it comes from an ocean, a lake, or a pool full of teenagers.

Celeste earned her driver's license that January and was eager to start driving our car on her own. I was fine with that during the day, but I was tough about her driving at night. I did not want my sixteen year old daughter all alone, at night, on a dark road at 9 PM. Celeste wasn't happy about this rule, but another part of her seemed to enjoy having me watch her practice during the evening hours. During practice I had little to say and stayed out of the way. I just maintained my role as "driver." Now and again I would catch her looking into the stands to see if I was still there. I was always there, smiling back at her, usually holding a good book in my hands.

I enjoyed the camaraderie that this new team had with one another. One mother, who had been instrumental in starting the team, came over and introduced herself one evening. It was through her that I met more and more of the parent group. As I got to know them, I found myself liking them all. I tried to avoid telling them about Celeste's bullying experiences, but when asked, I briefly described the bullying that had taken place. I wanted them to know why we were driving all the way from another city to be on this team. The parents who heard our story seemed horrified that anything like that could happen. I remember one gracious mother saying, "Celeste is such a lovely addition to our team."

What a relief to hear these kind words. We had been hated, maligned and attacked by angry people in our former situation; but, this new group seemed kind and caring. I felt like we had hit the swim team "jackpot" for sure.

Celeste and I found ourselves enjoying happier days than we had known in months. She loved her new high school and was making many new friends. At last, it appeared that this new USS team was a perfect fit for both of us. Unknown to us, however, there were challenges ahead. When the time came for another USS sanctioned meet, she would once again be face to face with all of the bullies from her old team. This would force me to "manage" the anger that I still felt about the situation we had just left behind.

Whether we liked it or not, the next USS meet was fast approaching and both of us were a little nervous. We found solace in the fact that we would have a new group to sit with, and the opportunity to be safely "sheltered" under the canopy with her new team.

When the weekend of the USS meet finally arrived, I was full of mixed emotions. I was happy to be part of our new loving parent-swimmer group; but, I knew it would not be an easy transition for either of us. The bullies from her former team would be waiting!

I tried to prepare my daughter by asking her to always be mindful of what was happening around her. "Situational Awareness," is what is needed when entering a place where danger may lurk.

Friday arrived and I settled in with the new group of parents as we prepared for the day. Sure enough, the first "attempt" to derail my daughter occurred in the locker room. The same old group of bullies surrounded her with a bevy of threats and negative remarks. She quickly left the locker room and hurried over to speak with me, "Mom. I can't even change in there. It's not safe."

My response? "Oh yes you can. Let's go."

I accompanied her into the locker room and sat on a bench as my daughter changed into her racing suit. Bullies scattered like flies leaving the two of us alone: they were still afraid of me and that was a good thing. Once again it had become apparent that bullies tend to behave as "pack animals." Like a pack of wolves, they find their strength in the company of other wolves. Anytime Celeste faced any of them alone, she had the upper hand. Sadly, they always seemed to travel in a group which further frustrated my daughter.

After the locker room episode, Celeste was fine as she sat chatting with her new teammates. It was only minutes before it was time for her to swim her first race, the 200 freestyle. I watched the bully group gather at the end of her swim lane! I knew what they planned to do… taunt and chide her as she made her turns at the wall. Celeste glanced my way when she saw them from her place on the starting blocks. I nodded at her as if to say "Watch this."

I quickly walked over and stood at the end of her lane. Immediately upon arriving, the bully group scattered. I thought to myself, "This is going to get very old, having to be my child's bodyguard at all these meets." As time consuming as bodyguard would be, I was not about to allow the bully group to get in the way of my child's performance.

When Celeste took her position for the start, she looked relieved to see me standing at the end of her lane. Bang! The starting gun rang out. I could see that she was quickly off the blocks with a good start. Each time she made a flip-turn at the end of her lane she could see me confidently smiling at her. When she finished her race, I strolled back to my seat. The mother sitting next to me looked confused. I said, "It's pretty bad when you have to be a bodyguard so your child isn't harassed while she is swimming."

I went on to say, "That's why we are here. I had to get her away from a petty group of her old teammates who wanted to see Celeste fail." The mother still looked confused, but I let it go at that.

This became our new routine; I would stand guard while my daughter changed in the locker room and when she swam her races. I knew her coach had other swimmers to watch and would not be able to keep her from being harmed. I truly didn't expect him to understand all of the problems we had experienced, but I did expect him to coach her properly.

In the beginning, the head coach was very enthusiastic about Celeste's swimming. She was so close to making her National qualifying times, and he wanted to be the one to help her get there. He would be taking a number of swimmers to a USS National Meet very soon and there was one spot left on the girl's relay team. The swimmers' performances at the summer finals would determine who would be going to this important meet. I was hoping that her coach would fill the slot with Celeste and give her some relief from her tormenters. I knew Celeste would be "safe" during the trip because no one in the bully group was fast enough to hold National times.

In the meantime, I had volunteered for the job of team "sports writer." It was the least I could do for this new group of warm and friendly people. At the end of each meet, I would gather the swimmers' final scores, wrap a little story around them, and send the articles to local papers and one national magazine called *Swimmer's World*. I was very busy at all the meets, making sure my child was safe from harassment while acting as the team's sports writer.

After a long summer of competition, the last meet arrived. I was standing in the direct sun on a very hot summer day, gathering swimmers' times for an article when her coach approached me by the score board area. He said, "Celeste just swam the 50 freestyle posting the fastest time between the two girls I was considering for the empty relay spot. Celeste will be going with us to the Nationals!"

As I shook his hand and thanked him for his fine coaching skills he continued, "Mrs. Wood, it was Celeste who made it happen and not me."

Yes! After all this time, effort and expense, my daughter would attend a National meet! She would be with her new team, competing against the finest swimmers in the nation. I was thrilled as I looked around to find her but, she found me first. "Mom! Did you hear? I get to go with the team to the Nationals!"

I hugged her as we shared a private moment of pure joy. I was so happy that she would be visiting another part of our United States. Even more, I was thankful she would be with this new group of fine young swimmers.

There were lots of preparations to be made before they left. I learned that a local swimming sports store would be providing free "paper suits" for all of the swimmers. Paper suits were very expensive and I was glad I would be spared this expense. A paper suit is a very tight and close fitting suit, the closest thing to "skin" that you can buy. The first time I saw the girls wearing one of these suits my maternal instincts kicked in. I wanted to run around covering everyone up with a towel! The advantage of these suits is that they provide less "drag" in the water. Since an advantage of one-hundredth of a second can determine winning or losing, any drag-reducing agent is highly valued. When I came to understand this, my modesty fell by the wayside. I found comfort in the fact that each one of them was an elite athlete and this is what they wore.

The final touches on the matching jackets and pants the team would wear were being finished by a seamstress so that all the swimmers could be easily identified as a National team from our state. When the warmup suits were ready, Celeste brought her treasures home. When I saw my daughter's name engraved on her jacket, with "National Team" underneath, I had a private moment of complete emotion. I just let the tears fall. Celeste had come so far from those first days as an eleven-year-old neophyte to a Junior National Team participant. It was her hard work in the pool that had earned her this honor. I wondered if any of the other parents were having "motherhood" or "fatherhood" moments as they prepared their children for travel to the Junior National Championships.

When the day arrived for the team to travel, several of the parents were accompanying the team as chaperones. I had not volunteered because I wanted Celeste to literally "fly" on her own. As much as I wanted to see her swim at the Junior Nationals, I wanted her to have fun and be "herself." I knew that having Mom there would interfere, plus, the travel expense of an airplane ticket was considerable.

Those of us who stayed behind had our cameras ready at the airport, even though our swimmers feigned annoyance at having their pictures taken. It was a colorful group! The combination of matching team outfits with "National Team" embroidered on their jackets, and matching swim bags, formed a colorful picture that caused

## Chapter 14: Junior Nationals

people catching other flights to ask who they were! We proudly explained that their coach was taking them to the Junior National Swimming Championships.

As they called the passengers to board the plane, another mother and I wiped a tear from our eyes as we experienced a feeling of collective pride. I gave my daughter a big hug. After a second or two she turned and headed down the concourse with the rest of her team. I strained to see her before she turned a corner and out of sight. She looked back at me, gave a little smile and wave, and then disappeared on her way to the aircraft. What she didn't know was that I had hidden a card in her luggage wishing her all the best. If I couldn't be there to watch her swim, I could be there in spirit.

The parents watched until the plane took off. Then, we all made our way out of the airport to what remained of the day. As I drove home alone I missed my little swimmer, but I knew she was on her way to a big adventure. Traveling alone would help her mature, and I was already looking forward to hearing her stories when she returned.

## Chapter Fifteen
# Facing Weighty Issues

CELESTE PERFORMED WELL at the Nationals, as did all of the swimmers on her USS team. I was pleased to hear about all of the interesting things they saw and experienced. I was particularly grateful to their coaches for giving them several adventures away from the pool. The team saw a professional baseball game and they visited several museums and trendy restaurants.

Still, Celeste's personal National times remained elusive. She was only "hundredths" of a second from making her national qualifying times in both the 50 and 100 freestyle events. I knew it was frustrating for her as well as the head coach, but it had never mattered to me if she did make her times. I felt it was more important for her to travel to new places and enjoy what other cities had to offer. Our little family had not taken as many trips as I had hoped, so I knew that going to the "away" meets would give her a more worldly view of life in general.

As time went along, I could see that the pressure being put upon Celeste was beginning to take a personal toll. She was tired of trying so hard and having her coaches feel disappointed with her performance. I felt I needed to fill a new role in her life as a "success coach." I could see the look on the head coach's face when she failed to make her times again and again. He rarely smiled or even spoke to her after a race. Because of this lack of positive feedback I became her personal "cheerleader," reminding her she was doing her best and should be proud of herself for even competing.

At the beginning of Celeste's junior year, a new high school opened in Gilmore. Because of where we were "renting," Celeste was scheduled to be transferred. The sophomores and juniors from Gilmore High would be moved to the new school, while the senior class would stay at the original Gilmore High School. One positive thing about the new school was that it was closer to our home, so driving time would be reduced to and from the new campus. It also meant that Celeste's group would be the first graduating class from the new high school the following year.

Once Celeste moved into her new school and settled into another new routine, she felt pressure to join the high school swim team along with her friends. She did not want to disappoint her peer group, so her father and I decided to let her swim for her new school in addition to continuing with her USS team. In years past, the high school coaches only required the USS swimmers to train twice a week, knowing that those swimmers trained hard elsewhere the rest of the week. However, Celeste's new high school coach implemented a new rule. If a swimmer wanted to swim for the new high school, he or she had to attend every after-school practice, five days a week. That would have been fine with me, except I knew that Celeste's USS Coach expected her to practice at the university pool every evening as well.

As a parent, I was once again concerned with the demands being placed upon my child. I knew this was too much time in the pool, but I did not want to make "waves" with any of the new coaches or teams. We reluctantly went along with this plan; but, as I expected, this new level of exhausting practice ultimately backfired in a big way. Obeying the rules of the high school coach, I picked my daughter up after high school practice, and we drove straight to the university pool so she could practice some more at night. I always had something in the car for Celeste to eat, but she refused to eat too much saying she didn't feel good in the water at the evening practice if she had just eaten.

As the high school swim season progressed, I began to see my child's figure change. My formerly "robust" swimmer was becoming thinner and thinner before my eyes. She had always been "fit," but her fitness was slowly morphing into "skinny."

Celeste helped win many meets that season for her new school. But, her times did not improve. I knew this was due to a lack of body fat. As is generally known, if a body lacks fat it has no energy "reserves" for peak performance.

I kept my concerns about Celeste's weight to myself, thinking I could help her get back to a normal weight after the high school swim season was over. As the season progressed, Celeste's new high school team worked their way to the 4A State Championships. Her new high school competed at the 4A level (rather than the 5A level) because of the relatively small number of students in the school. This meant that her new school would compete with smaller teams from around the state. The good news was that the bully group from her former 5A high school would compete at a different state meet on a different weekend.

She performed well at the 4A High School Championships. She swam as anchor on the relays and placed in the top five in two races. At the parent-swimmer banquet, she was awarded the Most Valuable Girl Trophy once again. I was happy for her, but I was more concerned with her shrinking figure. I knew that eating disorders were very common among elite athletes who had to maintain a careful balance between body weight and body strength. Swimming is one of the sports that is very sensitive to this balance, since hundredths-of-a-second often determine the difference between "the thrill of victory or the agony of defeat."

After the high school swim season came to an end, the continuous pressure of excessive practice with two swim teams caused her semester grades to fall. I understood why, and I spoke with her again on the importance

## Chapter 15: Facing Weighty Issues

of keeping her grade point average up for college admission. Since she no longer had to swim right after school, I encouraged her to take advantage of this opportunity to study before the evening USS practice began.

As Celeste continued to swim with her USS team, she had the opportunity to travel to several more locations throughout the United States with the National Team. Still, her personal best times were not improving and I could see that the head coach's attitude toward her was changing even more.

From my perspective, her "qualifying times" were not my concern. My "concern" was my daughter's ever diminishing physical size. She was losing more and more weight even though I filled her plate at mealtimes. After each meal I found most of her food left uneaten. I can remember pleading with her to eat more, but she refused.

She began wearing baggy clothes which I felt sure was a sign of an eating problem. I had read that many individuals with an eating disorder do not want others to know how small they have become, so they hide their figure beneath layers of clothing.

However, Celeste could not keep her figure hidden from me when she was in a swim suit. I remember being close to tears the day I saw her entire backbone and ribs pushing against her skin while she was getting ready to swim a backstroke event. I felt helpless, scared and alone once again.

Meanwhile, I was reading every book I could find on how to meet the nutritional needs of an elite athlete. My goal was to increase caloric intake at every meal.

As a precaution, I made a trip to my personal physician voicing my concerns about Celeste's weight. He insisted there was nothing we could do until her weight fell below ninety pounds.

My new focus was on helping my child stay well and return to a normal weight. Part of me wanted to pull her out of swimming entirely; but I knew she would miss all of her teammates too much, many of whom had become her best friends.

While she was practicing at night, I would slip away to buy some Ensure, i.e., a special mixture of nutrients, protein, vitamins, and minerals, to mix into her milkshakes when we returned home. Fortunately, Celeste loved ice cream! Even though I couldn't get her to eat a big meal, I was getting vitamins and minerals into her on a daily basis. I openly shared my concerns with Ben, but he had a way of ignoring or downplaying anything which concerned me. Once again, I felt alone, with the responsibility for my child's health and well-being resting squarely on my shoulders.

I learned to take one day at a time and tried not to "what if" myself too often. What if I had never let her join the first swim team? What if she had stayed in the dance program (notorious for generating eating disorders)? What if I had just let her get an after-school job?

When my mind would wander into the land of "what if's," I tried my best to think of other things. In the meantime, I focused on driving my tiny daughter from city to city, buying more and more Ensure to "ensure" that she had the energy needed for competition.

## Chapter Sixteen
# Transition

CELESTE'S WEIGHT LOSS had become a point of contention between the two of us. As much as I was trying to prepare healthy meals with lots of great things to eat, she was not particularly interested. We had "words" at times because I may have been pushing the "food" thing too hard. As a last resort, I was still making a lot of milkshakes, spiked with Ensure that she couldn't turn down.

It caused me great pain to see her get so thin. I shared my fears with no one, but I am sure her team members noticed her getting thinner and thinner. Even a young man she was dating tried to get her to eat more but it fell on deaf ears.

The summer after her junior year, it seemed that Celeste was intentionally sabotaging herself and her skill in the pool. It may not have been a conscious effort, but I believe that at a subconscious level she was thinking that if she lost enough weight, she could not be expected to improve her times and the head coach would leave her alone. Sure enough, it worked. She and the head coach now avoided one another during practice and at meets. She knew she had disappointed him, and he chose to ignore her rather than vent his obvious anger.

As Celeste's mother, I found myself in-between them, just wishing they could get along even though I knew it was not going to happen. A complete "disconnect" had taken place between the two of them: It was as if Celeste had become a "ghost" on the team. She simply didn't exist anymore in his eyes.

Anytime her team competed against the old bully group, they continued to take advantage of the situation by stepping up their harassment. As a result, I still stood guard in the locker room and on the kool deck during Celeste's races. I thought to myself, "At least I only have one more year of this and then they will all go to college or off to work."

I was beginning to concern myself with where this group of problem children would be going to college. Wherever they went, I wanted my daughter to attend school as far away as I could get her to go. We had already decided, as a family, that Celeste would not swim on a college team even though she was beginning to receive scholarship invitations from some of the smaller schools. We definitely felt a sense of accomplishment when we received letters from the collegiate swim coaches; however, Celeste was already experiencing the stress of trying to be an athlete while maintaining a high grade point average. I knew this would be even more difficult in a college environment. We all agreed that she had endured enough of this kind of stress and her tiny physique was a daily reminder.

As the hot summer days moved toward fall, I let her spend as much time with her friends as I could. When she wasn't swimming, she was having fun with both her team friends and friends from school. As a result, I was spending more and more time alone with an "absent" teenager. It was a tough time for me, but it was a necessary part of preparing both of us for her eventual "departure" to college and beyond. I simply focused on other things that I liked to do, and tried not to worry about her or her weight too much. Her senior year in high school was quickly approaching and I knew that my time with her was fleeting at best.

As the summer came to a close, Celeste's times were still not improving and she was not anchoring as many relays as before. The coach was putting other swimmers in her place causing Celeste and me to become complacent about the whole situation. I continued to support her at meets by being her cheerleader, bodyguard and success coach; but, I began to wonder how long either of us could continue this charade. Still, it seemed pointless to walk away from the whole swimming environment. We had come this far, why not finish the last year with a USS team? Once this was accomplished she could move on: it was only a short time until Celeste would be creating a new life in college with new classes and new friends. It would be her time to renew herself, face new challenges and begin another exciting chapter in her life.

## Chapter Seventeen

# *Senior Year*

Our family spent some time vacationing on the California coast before returning home for Celeste's senior year. We had agreed that Celeste would not swim for her high school team again, although she would continue with her USS team. As parents, our greatest concern was for both her physical and her mental health. I was not going to allow the "system" to physically abuse my child by forcing her into extreme practice in the pool again.

There was also a concern for her grade point average. Celeste had been successful in increasing her grades to a solid B average. That improvement, along with her test scores and teacher recommendations, would allow her to attend any of the state universities. As parents, we were content with that fact.

Since I had really been the "resident" parent during this entire swimming ordeal, I decided it was time for my husband Ben to get involved. His job was to deliver the unpleasant news to the high school coach: Celeste would not be returning to high school swimming during her senior year. I knew if Celeste approached her coach with this message she would probably be harassed the rest of her senior year. If her father delivered the news, it would more likely mean "end of topic."

I knew that Ben was not happy about having to do this "deed." My thinking was that a coach would respond less emotionally when dealing with a man. With this in mind, I sent Ben to the first high school practice alone while Celeste and I stayed home and waited to see what would happen.

As I imagined, the high school coach was shocked at the news, then angry, then accepting of the fact that we, as a family, were not going to put our swimmer through a combination of high school and USS club training again. Ben used the "drop" in her grade point average as the reason for her not returning to the team. The fact that she was rail thin never entered the conversation. For some reason, many men hesitate discussing such personal issues. Regardless, it would have fallen on deaf ears. I had learned that the bottom line for any coach was winning races. It caused me deep sadness to realize that that my daughter's shrinking figure didn't seem to matter to anyone but me! I wondered how professional coaches could ignore the obvious fact that an athlete had become frail, and had lost the "zest" for the sport

## Chapter 17: Senior Year

she once loved. It appeared that many coaches were so focused on winning that they never noticed or cared.

Even though Celeste was no longer a member of the team, she was able to remain friends with several of her high school swim friends. Many of them may have been glad she did not return because it gave them the chance to be a "star." The same was not true, however, with the high school swimming coach. This individual chose to remain angry throughout the year. Regardless, Celeste ignored the bad attitude and angry glares in the hallways. She concentrated on her studies knowing they would contribute to her acceptance into one of the three state schools she wanted to attend. She had applied to all three schools so she could select a school where the bullies were not attending. I knew I could get the information we needed to carry out this avoidance strategy. Like all special-interest groups, the swimming community was small even though we lived in a major metropolitan area.

Celeste's senior year seemed to go by too fast. I knew I was going to miss my daughter terribly when she went away to college. When I attended college, I chose a school that was two states away from my family home. In retrospect, it was a healthy decision because it helped me mature in ways that have been beneficial throughout my life. Few would disagree that the ability to problem solve, with no parental input, is crucial for maturity. I wanted that for my daughter.

Celeste graduated the following spring with a solid B+ average and was accepted to all three state universities. We did indeed find out where the members of the bully group planned to attend college. Several chose to continue their education in the northern part of the state: only one planned to continue team swimming...as a "walk on." That meant that she was not offered swimming scholarship.

As I looked back on the eight years of swimming experience that led to this point, I was shocked to realize that we endured so much "hassle" for no good reason. Celeste was never a clear threat to any of the bully group; they simply chose to torment her. I took a deep sigh when I realized that this hurtful, selfish behavior would soon be coming to an end. Plans were underway to send our daughter to a college in the southern part of the state. This would put Celeste and the old bully group five hours apart. At last, distance and time would allow our daughter to heal and grow into adulthood.

As Celeste's senior year spun down, one final moment of pain had to be endured in the name of competitive swimming. Celeste's father, as always, seemed immune; but my child and I felt it full force.

It took place just before the Summer Junior Nationals that were being held in our state for the first time. She was excited about the opportunity to swim at the Nationals because expensive travel was not required, and she would have an opportunity to once again swim against the best swimmers in the United States.

I made certain that Celeste's warmup outfit was washed and ready for the fast approaching meet. It would be the first time in all of her years of swimming that I would have the opportunity to watch her compete at the Junior National level. I was looking forward to that proud moment when her team would march in to huge applause as they took their places for the competition. My daughter had earned a spot on the team and I would be one proud mom, cheering for her and her National teammates. In my mind it would be a "mini" Olympic moment.

Several weeks before the Junior National meet, Celeste swam in several events at a USS Club meet. I didn't expect any time-shattering performances because she was still very thin and didn't have the stamina she once had in the pool. In addition, she was four years older than when she had taken the state by storm as a freshman. With all of this in mind, I would be content to know that she gave each race her best effort. That is all I ever required. Before each race, my message was always: "Just do the best you can!"

As the USS Club meet was coming to an end on that Sunday afternoon, and I was beginning to pack up our things, a mother from our team ran up to me with a very excited look on her face. With great exuberance she exclaimed, "Leslie! The head coach just put Colleen on the relay for the upcoming Junior National meet! Isn't that wonderful?"

Surprised, I said, "Great! I am so happy for you and your daughter!"

As she raced away to make this announcement to some other parents, the news hit me like someone had thrown a bucket of water in my face. Stunned, it suddenly occurred to me that the coach was replacing my daughter with Colleen. My Celeste was being pulled off the National Team so that a slower swimmer could participate. I felt sick, and wondered how long it would take for Celeste to find out the news. She was being replaced, thrown away, for the last National meet for which she was qualified.

I continued to gather up our towels and swim gear trying not to show any emotion. This seemed like a cruel injustice to me: Celeste had worked so hard, tiny body and all, to qualify for the Nationals. Her personal best times had not improved for awhile, but she was still one of the top free-style swimmers in the state.

Looking back, I feel the coaches did not make the decision to replace Celeste with any mal-intent. I can only think that because Celeste had failed to improve her times, they replaced her with a younger girl whom they thought was deserving of a spot on the relay teams.

As I visualized "the new girl" receiving her brand new warm-up suit and paper swim suits, I had to cope with the fact that Celeste and I would be putting her "National" items away, never to be used again. My heart felt like it was breaking into a million pieces. I experienced the sickening mixture of emotions; anger, betrayal, sadness and grief. I wanted to leave the pool as soon as possible where I could be alone with my feelings.

Just then, Celeste walked up to me. The tears in her eyes made me tear up too. She asked, "Did you hear the news?"

With a heavy heart I said, "Yes. Let's go home."

## Chapter 17: Senior Year

She helped me gather the rest of our things as we headed toward the car. My tears were falling like a summer rain storm. One of my closer "mom" friends stopped me just before we got in the car. She caught me crying and said, "Oh, Leslie. I am so sorry. I don't know how this could have happened!"

This woman's daughter was the most gifted swimmer on the team, and this kind lady was offering me sympathy. I just nodded my head and said nothing. She knew it was best to leave it at that and she walked away.

Celeste and I closed the doors to the car, locked them, and let the tears flow. We sat in the darkness of the car and watched the other cars leave the parking lot. I let the "floodwaters" quietly continue. Celeste "dried up" before I did and asked, "Mom, do you want me to drive home?"

I said, "No. Driving will force me to stop this crying nonsense."

We drove along in silence with nothing to say. Silence seemed to be our best friend on that very painful night.

## Chapter Eighteen
# New Beginnings

THE JUNIOR NATIONAL CHAMPIONSHIPS came and went that summer without Celeste's participation. Our daughter would end her swimming career that summer after swimming in the final USS State Meet. She would then move on to her new life as a young college student with all of the challenges and fun that college life offered.

One day, when Celeste was out with a friend, I quietly packed up her National Swim Team items. She never asked me what I did with them and I never found a reason to tell her. Twenty years later, I still have that box of National Swim Team items under one of the beds in my guest room. Twenty years from now they may still be there. I have never looked at them again because it still causes me pain even thinking about the series of events that caused so much unnecessary sadness.

I supported my daughter throughout the rest of the summer as we attended local USS meets and those that were held out of town. I almost found it humorous that the head coach was still using Celeste as the anchor on the relays even though he had taken her off the National Team. One huge lesson I learned from these experiences was to be prepared for "change." It was part of life, and it was certainly a part of Celeste's participation in the world of swimming.

When we attended the meets, the bully group was still around, but college plans and new beginnings were keeping them busy. They had less time to bother Celeste and we liked it that way. Regardless, I never stopped my vigilant surveillance even though they seemed to ease up as the summer progressed.

One night, when we were driving home from a late-night summer meet, Celeste became quiet. This caused me some concern because she was usually quite talkative after swimming so hard. I would drive, and she would talk with me quite openly about any number of topics. In fact, she would often blurt out something she knew I wouldn't like because she felt it was a safe thing to do while I was driving. After all, if I was driving 65 MPH down a freeway, it would be dangerous to react negatively to what she was saying!

Her silence seemed to go on forever when she finally said, "Mom, I want to thank you."

As I eased my car past a semi-truck on the freeway I asked, "For what?"

## Chapter 18: New Beginnings

"For doing what you did to keep me safe. I will always be grateful for having a mother like you."

Her words touched a deep place in my heart. A parent never expects to hear "thank you" from a child; when it happens it stirs deep feelings of emotion. I simply replied, "I did what I did because I love you so much. I followed my instincts and did what I felt was necessary to keep you safe from harm. It's what any mother would do for her beloved child."

The last meet of the summer was held at the university where Celeste would be attending college: it was fun to finish her swimming career at that excellent pool. Even though she would not be part of the college team, I stood at the rail and visualized her working out in the pool during "free swim" hours. I knew the university had a Master's program for older swimmers who still loved competition and I hoped she would join this group if she wished to do so.

It didn't seem long until it was time for Celeste's last relay of her last meet. Celeste was the anchor, and the last to swim as she had done so many times before. One of my good mom friends stood at the end of the pool to watch the race with me. As Celeste took off from the blocks, swam her laps and went into her final flip turn, my friend turned to me and said these exact words, "No one looks more beautiful in the pool than Celeste. She is grace in motion."

I looked at my friend and smiled. Then, I focused on the swimmers as they approached the finish line. My friend had certainly nailed her description of Celeste as I watched her move through the water…she truly was grace in motion. In what seemed only a moment the race was over. She did it! I felt a sense of deep pride as I watched my athletic daughter bring in the relay for her team's final "win" of the season.

### Chapter Nineteen

# Lessons Learned

*"Bullies are losers not winners.
Don't give your power to a loser."*
— Virginia Kuwahara

I<small>N THIS FINAL CHAPTER</small>, I have summarized some of the more important lessons Celeste and I learned as we made our way through the bullying described in this story. Although my experience came as a mother trying to protect her child, there are a number of "lessons learned" that can apply to any situation where bullying is involved. This includes teachers, coaches, administrators, law enforcement, and any adults or young people being bullied for any reason. Hopefully, our experiences can benefit anyone who is somehow involved in this unnecessary, demeaning, and sometimes fatal behavior.

- *"Shortstop" bullying as soon as possible.* Don't be bashful and don't "give your power away" by assuming the problem will go away. Speak to the appropriate teachers, coaches, administrators or law enforcement personnel. If lower levels of authority do not appear to be listening, keep moving to higher levels until something positive is done or you run out of options.

- *Acknowledge the possibility of gang behavior if multiple individuals are involved.* Although one person can act as a bully, bullying can often become a type of "gang" activity. As with all types of gang behavior, the potential for damage increases as members reinforce each other's bad behavior. However, when the gang is dissolved, former individual gang members seldom "act out" on their own. For this reason, acknowledge the group aspect of bullying and attack it from this perspective.

- *Keep your lines of communication open.* Do your best to know what's going on in the minds of your children or loved ones. Watch their "silent language" as well as their "spoken language." Are they happy? Are they forthcoming in their conversations with you? Are they withdrawn? Put it all together and "know your child."

  In the same vein, try your best to know your children's best friends and their parents. The old

### Chapter 19: Lessons Learned

saying that "You become like the people you associate with" is particularly true for young people as they work through the process of becoming adults.

If it should ever appear that your child is acting as a bully rather than being bullied, take action to correct this behavior immediately.

➤ *Be a good sport whether a parent or an athlete.* As a parent, be a good sport and guard against personal desires such as obtaining family fame, saving money through scholarships or finding pleasure in accomplishments you wish you had achieved.

As an athlete, put the Golden Rule into effect by treating others like you want to be treated. Be their friend, compliment them when they win, and study their winning ways so you can do the same.

➤ *Expect jealousy and possible loss of friends when you are a "winner."* The process of winning, as well as the symbols of success, can provoke jealousy. Examples include letterman's jackets, trophies, and other related awards. Unfortunately, jealousy seems to be a part of human behavior. When the decision is made to compete, be ready to experience jealousy toward you when you win…it's a part of the competition process. If you experience jealousy yourself, do what champions do: study the winners and turn your feeling of jealousy into a motivation to perform better than they do.

- *Acknowledge the importance of peer groups for teenagers.* Bullying becomes an important problem when it results in a feeling of isolation. All of us want to have friends and feel like we are part of their lives. This is true not only in sports but throughout the fabric of life. For this reason, the feeling of isolation that can come from being bullied is a high-priority problem. Never down-play the seriousness of bullying by simply accepting it as a normal way of life. Taken to its greatest extreme, a feeling of isolation is so painful that suicide seems the only answer. You may have experienced bullying and survived: your loved one may not.

- *Recognize the "two-edged sword" of combating bullying.* Parents or family members must be sensitive to *when* to become involved and *how* to proceed. An obvious goal is to contain (or manage) the bullying without increasing it. As suggested in this book, work the problem through several stages. Begin by knowing the feelings of your child or loved one and make every effort to keep your lines of communication open. Always try to be ahead of the bullying process. Anytime bullying is evident, offer counseling on how to manage the problem. If the bullying reaches a point where it is interfering with an individual's everyday life, seek assistance from any source that can help. This

## Chapter 19: Lessons Learned

includes professional psychological help as well as local law enforcement agencies.

- *Enlist "Dad" in the bullying control process.* Since dads are often working and not present when or where the bullying is taking place, it often falls to mom to take on the "bullying control" process. Since the male presence of "dad" is often given more attention than "mom," a strong father figure can often have decisive impact on the bully control process. When it appears that mom's efforts are not effective, let an unhappy dad take over giving the signal that enough is enough.

- *Don't be surprised if your children's coaches use coaching techniques often used in professional sports.* Many times I observed swim coaches aggressively yelling at their swimmers or taking an opposite approach with the so called "silent treatment." They were also "benched," or taken off trips with the intended goal of motivating the swimmers to higher levels of achievement. Although this is standard practice in professional sports, and can be defended as a motivational tool or selection process, it often backfired with the children I observed. Rather than being a motivating force, it often took a young athlete's joy out of performing. As a result, what was intended to be motivating was, in fact, discouraging. This resulted in poorer performance or even a desire to leave the program entirely.

➤ *Speak with coaches and teachers, even if they do not appear to respond to your concerns.* It's discouraging when officials are contacted and nothing seems to change. This can happen for several reasons: (a) there are no formal rules regarding bullying, (b) bullying is expected to be "worked out" by the students themselves, (c) the bullying occurs during after-school activities, or (d) the school staff fears enraging the bully's parents. Regardless, let the bullying be known. Your complaints can pave the way for future action.

➤ *Support your children when possible by attending competitions and appearing interested.* After a hard day at work, it's very tempting to drop into an easy chair and watch your favorite TV program; however, take a hot shower, put on some fresh clothes and spend the time it takes to watch your children perform. From your child's perspective, your extra effort shows your young athlete that they are important to you and that you are excited by their accomplishments. It also gives you an opportunity to observe the overall competitive environment. Is your child melding with the other team members and is your child having fun? How are the coaches and other officials behaving? This is an opportunity to be "tuned in" and to see, first-hand, what your child's life is like during competition.

## Chapter 19: Lessons Learned

It should be remembered that the general psychological literature shows that neglectful, biased parents are more likely to raise children who demonstrate bullying behavior. Data suggests that when a child's parents show little concern for how they behave or what is important to them, the child will tend to abuse others when no authority figure is around. Once initiated, the child's bullying behavior may be planned or unplanned, often resulting in the recruitment of other children in a gang-like fashion.

> *Realize that bully parents can be as much a problem as their bully children.* This is definitely a warning, and one that this real-life story encountered but did not elaborate. Be aware that the actions of a bully child may be reflecting the bully attitudes of the child's parents. This is certainly a complicating factor, but one that is open to one-on-one adult confrontation and hopefully an adult-based solution. What has become known as a parents' "Little League" attitude is apparent in all sports, swimming included. In a worst case situation, where all efforts to ignore or counteract bullying have proven ineffective, make the bullying known and hope that formal options are in place to bring it under control. If "formal options" are not available, become an activist for bully control and help give teachers, coaches and law enforcement the

tools they need to stop this senseless attack on those who would bring others down to their own level of inadequacy.

➢ *Shortstop cyber-bullying.* In years past, before texting and social media, bullying primarily took place on a one-on-one basis. Today, bullying can follow a target wherever he or she may go; traveling in a car, sitting in a restaurant or in the dark privacy of one's own bedroom. Cyber-bullying involves a complex array of issues that are slowly being addressed by a number of organizations, businesses and agencies. As concerned parents, teachers or administrators, we must make sure that (1) we are sensitive to cyber-bullying when it is taking place, and (2) that we actively seek out and support ways to combat cyber-bullying when it becomes a problem. Hopefully, good progress will be seen in this area as everyone comes together to solve the many issues involved.

➢ *Goals for the future:* Social scientists have long known that the quality of a society is strongly based on the strength and morality of the family unit. Without doubt the basic responsibility for a child's behavior rests firmly on the backs of the family, however "family" is defined. Although the overall quality of family life can not be legislated, every family-oriented educational source can have a positive impact; included are television, radio, social media, churches, parent teachers associations and any other form of communication aimed at the family unit.

Because the process of identifying bullies is complex, we must support research that strives to better understand the bullying process and to devise valid ways to detect both the bullies and the bullied. Given this information, all of the "players" in the school system, e.g., the teachers, counselors and coaches, must be given the guidelines, training and authority needed to counsel those involved. This will cost money and may even be perceived by some as an over-reach of power. However, most would admit that "freedom from fear" is a worthy American principle.

Finally, all top administrators must take the initiative to elevate bullying from "something that kids do" to "something that can kill." When bullying is put into the same categories as drunk driving and inappropriate use of firearms, only then will schools and law enforcement have the clout to bring bullying under control. In the meantime, those who are perceived as being a bit different in terms of their looks, their skills, their beliefs, or their sexual preferences will continue to be denigrated and harassed, reducing their quality of life to a level where taking their own lives is seen as an only option.

- *Need Help?* Every day, more and more resources are being made available to those who are being bullied or who are even contemplating thoughts of suicide. Two sources at this writing are:

  www.StopBullying.gov; and, (in the US) the National Suicide Prevention Lifeline at 1-800-273-8255.

## Chapter Twenty
# *Epilogue*

I CONSIDER MYSELF ONE OF the lucky ones. My daughter is still here; healthy, married, with a young son of her own.

Happily, Celeste completed college and is currently finishing her MBA. At the present time she is teaching middle-school science. This is an interesting turn of events because this is the same age group that bullied her relentlessly when she was a competitive swimmer.

What does she do when she sees anything indicative of bullying behavior in her classroom? She puts out the "bullying fire" immediately! Because of her experiences as a young competitive swimmer, she has instituted a "no tolerance policy" for bullying-type behavior in any of her classes. In fact, she not only squelches any evidence of bullying she observes, she is quick to counsel any student being bullied to help them manage the bullying process.

In Celeste's community, local law enforcement can and will get involved if they are made aware of a serious bullying situation. Anyone can call them on their non-emergency line, giving them any details that can assist their investigation. Usually, one visit from an armed police officer, with questions aimed directly at the bully or their parents, will put an immediate stop to the problem.

Twenty years ago bullying took place mostly on a one-to-one basis. There were no cell phones or social media like Facebook, Twitter or YouTube. Today, communication technology has made everyone open to visual, verbal or written bullying regardless of age, color or sexual preference. With the passage of time, communication technology will only increase the number of opportunities for bullying to take place. This will require even more vigilance by parents and loved ones to prevent the isolation, desperation and degradation that bullying can bring to otherwise normal individuals.

It is my greatest hope that our story has provided some insight into the bullying process and what to do about it. Although Celeste was just a child, the frustration, fear and loss of joy she experienced can be experienced by anyone.

As a parent or loved one, be proactive when you see the signs of bullying taking place.

If you are doing the bullying, knock it off! Do so, and you may save a life.

# Appendix

**Recent Research:**

The following studies represent recent research on various aspects of bullying. The reader is encouraged to explore this information-rich area using only a few clicks on your computer's browser.

**Ashbaugh, L., & Cornell, D. (2008). Sexual harassment and bullying behaviors in sixth graders.** *Journal of School Violence,* **7, 21–38.**

*Objective:* Explore sexual harassment as a form of middle-school bullying. (N=109)

*Results:* Boys and girls reported similar rates of harassment. Boys were more likely than girls to try to ignore sexual harassment, but girls were more likely to tell someone about their experience and to tell the perpetrator to stop.

**Branson, C., & Cornell, D. (2009). A comparison of self and peer reports in the assessment of middle school bullying.** *Journal of Applied School Psychology.* **25, 5–27.**

*Objective*: Explore the effectiveness of school-wide anti-bullying programs. (N=355)

*Results*: Concerns were raised about relying on self or peer reports alone to assess the prevalence of middle-school bullying.

**Brockenbrough, K., Cornell, D., & Loper, A. (2002). Aggressive victims of violence at school.** *Education and Treatment of Children,* **273–287.**

*Objective*: Assess how attitudes of aggression affect the behavior of victims and non-victims. (N=1090)

*Results*: Victims with aggressive attitudes were more likely to report they had carried weapons, used alcohol and engaged in physical fights at school. Both victims and non-victims with aggressive attitudes reported lower academic grades and fewer supportive adults at school than the nonaggressive attitude groups.

**Cole, J., Cornell, D., & Sheras, P. (2006). Identification of school bullies by survey methods.** *Professional School Counseling.*

*Objective*: Compare two methods of identifying middle-school bullies. (N=386)

*Results*: Peer nomination appears more effective at identifying school bullies rather than a reliance on student self-reports.

Cornell, D., & Bandyopadhyay, S. (2009). The assessment of bullying. In S. R. Jimerson, S. M. Swearer, & D. L. Espelage (Eds.). *The International Handbook of School Bullying.* New York: Routledge.

Cornell, D., & Brockenbrough, K. (2004). Identification of bullies and victims: A comparison of methods. *Journal of School Violence*, 63–87.

*Objective*: Compare self, peer and teacher identification of bullies and bully victims in a sample of middle-school students. (N=416)

*Results*: There was a poor correspondence between self-reports and reports made by peers or teachers; but, consistently better agreement between peers and teachers in identifying both bullies and victims of bullying.

Cornell, D, Sheras, P., & Cole, J. (2006). Assessment of bullying. In S.R. Jimerson & M.J. Furlong (Eds.). *The Handbook of School Violence and School Safety: From Research to Practice* (pp. 191–210).

Erlbaum, L., Thompson, W., & Cornell, D. (2007). Differences between persistent and desistent middle school bullies. *School Psychology International.*

*Objective*: Investigate differences in aggressive attitudes, academic achievement and discipline referrals between sixth and seventh grade bullies and non-bullies. (N=261)

*Results*: Across all students, aggressive attitudes were associated with poorer grades and more discipline infractions.

**Thunfors, P., & Cornell, D. (2008). The popularity of middle-school bullies. *Journal of School Violence*, 7, 65–82.**

*Objective*: Investigate the peer popularity of middle-school students involved in bullying. (N=379)

*Results*: Bullies were among the most popular students in the school, receiving more peer nominations on average (21) than students uninvolved in bullying (13) or victims (4).

**Unnever, J., & Cornell, D. G. (2003). Bullying, self-control, and ADHD. *Journal of Interpersonal Violence*, 18, 129–147.**

*Objective*: Investigate the influence of low self-control and Attention Deficit Hyperactivity Disorder (ADHD) on middle-school bullying and bully victimization. (N=1,315)

*Results*: Low self-control and ADHD were identified as potential risk factors for bullying and victimization.

**Unnever, J. & Cornell, D. (2003). The culture of bullying in middle school. *Journal of School Violence*, 2, 5–27.**

*Objective:* Assess the nature and extent of student attitudes toward bullying. (N=1,313)

*Results*: A culture of bullying is a pervasive phenomenon among middle-school students and should be an important consideration in bullying prevention efforts.

**Unnever, J. & Cornell, D. (2004). Middle-school victims of bullying: Who reports being bullied?** *Aggressive Behavior,* 30, 373–388.

*Objective:* Examine factors that influence a student's decision to report being bullied at school. (N=2,437)

*Results:* It was found that reporting was generally more frequent among girls than boys and among lower grade levels. Students were less likely to report being bullied if they perceived the school climate to be tolerant of bullying, as were students who received coercive (forced) discipline from their parents.

**Williams, F., & Cornell, D. (2006). Student willingness to seek help for threats of violence.** *Journal of School Violence,* 5, 35–49.

*Objective*: Examine factors that influence a middle-school student's willingness to seek help for a threat of violence. (N=542)

*Results*: Students who hold aggressive attitudes and perceive the school climate to be tolerant of bullying were less likely to seek help.

**The following excerpt,** *Effects of Bullying On Its Victims,* **was taken from an article by Missy Fleming, Ph.D. that reports findings presented during a May 3, 2002 American Medical Association sponsored "Educational Forum on Adolescent Health" that focused on "Youth Bullying."**

## Summary:

Bullying may seriously affect the psychosocial functioning, academic work and the physical health of children who are targeted. Bully victimization has been found to be related to lower self-esteem (Hodges & Perry, 1996; Olweus, 1978; Rigby & Slee, 1993), higher rates of depression (Craig, 1998; Hodges & Perry, 1996; Olweus, 1978; Rigby & Slee, 1993; Salmon et al., 2000; Slee, 1995), loneliness (Kochenderfer & Ladd, 1996; Nansel et al., 2001), and anxiety (Craig, 1998; Hodges & Perry, 1996; Olweus, 1978; Rigby & Slee, 1993). Victims are more likely to report wanting to avoid attending school (Kochenderfer & Ladd, 1996) and have higher school absenteeism rates (Rigby, 1996). Although more research is needed to assess health-related outcomes of bullying, researchers have identified that victims of bullying were more likely to report experiencing poorer general health (Rigby, 1996), have more migraine headaches (Metsähonkala, Silanpaa, & Tuomien, 1998), and report more suicidal ideation (Rigby, 1996) than their non-bullied peers. For example, in a study of Australian school children, those who reported being bullied at least once a week were twice as likely as their peers to "wish they were dead" or admit to having a recurring idea of taking their own life (Rigby, 1996).

## References for above:

Craig, W. M. (1998). The relationship among bullying, victimization, depression, anxiety, and aggression in elementary school children. *Personality & Individual Differences*, 24, 123–130.

Hodges, E. V. E., & Perry, D. G. (1996). Victims of peer abuse: An overview. *Journal of Emotional and Behavioural Problems, 5*, 23–28.

Kochenderfer, B. J., & Ladd, G. W. (1996). Peer victimization: Cause or consequence of school maladjustment? *Child Development, 67*, 1305–1317.

Metsähonkala, L., Sillanpää, M., & Tuominen, J., (1998). Social environment and headache in 8- to 9-year-old children: A follow-up study. *Headache, 38*, 222–228.

Nansel, T. R., Overpeck, M., Pilla, R. S., Ruan, W. J., SimonsMorton, B., & Scheidt, P. (2001). Bullying behavior among US youth: Prevalence and association with psychosocial adjustment. *Journal of the American Medical Association, 285*, 2094–2100.

Olweus, D. (1978). Aggression in the schools: bullies and whipping boys. Washington, DC: Wiley.

Rigby, K. (1996). Bullying in schools and what to do about it. Bristol, PA: Jessica Kingsley Publishers.

Rigby, K. & Slee, P. T. (1993). Dimensions of interpersonal relations among Australian school children and their implications for psychological well-being. *Journal of Social Psychology, 133*, 33–42.

Salmon, G., James, A., Cassidy, E. L., & Javoloyes, M. A. (2000). Bullying, a review: Presentations to an adolescent psychiatric service and within a school for emotionally and behaviorally disturbed children. *Clinical Child Psychology and Psychiatry, 5*, 563–579.

Slee, P. T. (1995). Peer victimization and its relationship to depression among Australian primary school students. *Personality and Individual Differences, 18,* 57–62.

CPSIA information can be obtained at www.ICGtesting.com
Printed in the USA
BVOW011855130612

292605BV00006B/17/P